At Eternity's Gate:
Artists of the Infinite

John O'Brien OFM

Other books by the author

Catch the Wind
Return to Gethsemane
My one Friend is Darkness
Rachel's Tears and Mary's Song
Love Rescue Me
Cry Me a River
Therese and the Little Way of Love and Healing
Clare of Assisi: A living Flame of Love
Waiting for God: From Trauma to Healing
With Thee Tender is the Night
Loneliness Knows My Name
Silent Music of Love: Teach Us to Pray

Front cover image: *The Return of the Prodigal Son* - by Rembrandt

To Máirtín and Sietske O'Connor

*"You are not a drop
in the ocean.*

*You are the entire ocean,
in a drop."*

~ Rumi ~

Contents

Introduction

We live in a world where violence, hate and greed seem to reign supreme. When Machiavelli wrote 'Il Principe' (The Prince) he wrote about how to be ruthless and succeed in life. The works of the righteous were all well and good but they didn't really have any relevance to "real life". John Steinbeck wrote in "The Log from the Sea of Cortez":

> "There is a strange duality in the human which makes for an ethical paradox. We have definitions of good qualities and of bad; not changing things, but generally considered good and bad throughout the ages and throughout the species. Of the good, we think always of wisdom, tolerance, kindliness, generosity, humility; and the qualities of cruelty, greed, self-interest, graspingness, and rapacity are universally considered undesirable. And yet in our structure of society, the so-called and considered good qualities are invariable concomitants of failure, while the bad ones are the cornerstones of success. A man – a viewing-point man – while he will love the abstract good qualities and detest the abstract bad, will nevertheless envy and admire the person who through possessing the abstract bad qualities has succeeded economically and socially, and will hold in contempt that person whose good qualities have caused failure. When such a viewing-point man thinks of Jesus or St. Augustine or Socrates he regards them with love because they are the symbols of the good he admires, and he hates the symbols of the bad. But actually he would rather be successful than good. In an animal other than man we would replace the term "good" with "weak survival quotient" and the term "bad" with "strong survival quotient". Thus, man in his thinking or reverie status admires the progression towards extinction, but in the unthinking stimulus which really activates him he tends toward survival. Perhaps no other animal is so torn between alternatives. Man might be described fairly adequately, if

simply, as a two-legged paradox. He has never become accustomed to the tragic miracle of consciousness. Perhaps, as has been suggested, his species is not set, has not jelled, but is still in a state of becoming, bound by his physical memories to a past of struggle and survival, limited in his futures by the uneasiness of thought and consciousness."

(John Steinbeck, The Log from the Sea of Cortez
[New York: 1951])

Soren Kierkegaard sought to make Christianity in his native Denmark more authentic. He saw the words of Scripture as being addressed to us personally. They contained a call for each individual. They were love letters from God. In more recent times Henri Nouwen sought to find spirituality in our world. He trained as a psychologist as well as a theologian. He had to battle against his own insecurities and failures. He spoke of these in his writings to give others courage in their struggles. He had to learn self-compassion and then compassion for others. Through his life and writings he enables us to find our 'home' in the love God has for us and allow that love to heal us. This is the journey we are on in this book. I deal with 'The Wall' by Pink Floyd. This shows us how we can get locked in on ourselves. It is love that breaks down the wall and we learn 'we are the Beloved of God'. In Chapter Three I look at Rembrandt's 'The Return of the Prodigal Son' and Henri's reflections on this painting. Then I look at Vincent Van Gogh and Henri's teaching based on Van Gogh to teach us compassion. The final chapter is based on Henri's shared meditations on four icons.

Chapter One

Homecoming:

St. Augustine said: "You have formed us for yourself, and our hearts are restless until they rest in you" (Confessions, Book 1). In our hearts there is an infinite longing. Augustine points out the fulfillment of that desire is in God. We get sidetracked looking at other people or things to satisfy the hunger in our hearts, but we end up disappointed. We can place too much on people to fill our needs – something no-one can do. Yet we are driven by the Spirit to always seek peace, "the peace that passes all understanding" (Philippians 4:7). This is the peace that comes when we know we are loved, accepted and forgiven. Finding God is our end, our purpose, our destiny, our peace our joy and home. He is the health of our soul. All our hearts are restless because we find ourselves in different places than our true home in God.

Finding our "rest":

In the Gospel of John we read:

> Turning around, Jesus saw them following and asked, "What do you want?" They said, "Rabbi" (which means "Teacher"), "where are you staying?" "Come," he replied, "and you will see." So they went and saw where he was staying, and they spent that day with him. It was about four in the afternoon.
>
> (Jn 1:38-39)

The verb used for 'staying' is *menein* in Greek. It can mean 'abiding' or 'dwelling' as we can see in various translations. The word works at different levels in the hands of John. Jesus is the Word made flesh (Jn 1:14). In the prologue we read:

In the beginning was the Word, and the Word was with God, and the Word was God. He was with God in the beginning. Through him all things were made; without him nothing was made that has been made. In him was life, and that life was the light of all mankind.

(John 1:1-4)

The phrase 'In the beginning' in verse 1 echoes Genesis 1:1 and alerts the reader to the idea of a new creation in the Gospel. The 'Word' (Logos) is present in the Old Testament as the creative energy of God, as in Genesis 1 and Isaiah 55. Logos was used to express in philosophy 'order', 'reason'. The Logos in John is the one through whom all things were created and who was with God and turned towards God even before creation. The 'Word made flesh', Jesus' true home is with the one he called 'Father'. Those who come to Jesus are introduced into fellowship with Jesus and the Father by the power of the Holy Spirit. John the Baptist sees the Holy Spirit 'abiding' on Jesus in Jn 1:32. The Holy Spirit dwells in Jesus.

In John 12:34 we read: "The crowd spoke up 'We have heard from the law that the Messiah will remain forever, so how can you say, 'The Son of Man must be lifted up'?'" Who is this 'Son of Man'? The verb *'menein'* is used here for 'remain forever'. In the Old Testament the abiding of God and the things and persons of God are of significance. As distinct from the mutability and transitoriness of everything earthly and human God is characterised by the fact he endures: His Word of address and promise abides (Isa 40:8), the new heaven and the new earth will remain (Isa 66:22), the new Jerusalem is the city which will know no destruction (Zech 14:10), divine wisdom remains and will make all things new (Wis 7:27), the righteous and their generation will share in God's abiding (Sir 44:13). Here in John the crowd cannot understand if Jesus is of God how can he suffer and die.

Yet Jesus would rise from the dead. As we saw John the Baptist saw the Holy Spirit dwelling on Jesus. This means Jesus is greater than the prophets who were honoured only with temporary inspiration. Jesus is filled with the Spirit and he pours out the Spirit on those who follow him. The giving of the Spirit is the endowment of Christians.

In Chapter 15 Jesus says:

> "I am the true vine, and my Father is the gardener. He cuts off every branch in me that bears no fruit, while every branch that does bear fruit he prunes so that it will be even more fruitful. You are already clean because of the word I have spoken to you. Remain in me, as I also remain in you. No branch can bear fruit by itself; it must remain in the vine. Neither can you bear fruit unless you remain in me."
>
> (John 15:1-4)

'Remain in me' or 'abide in me' is another example of *menein*. With Jesus we discover our true home with the Father. From the 'centre' of our lives we can reach out. Jesus had promised that he would always be present in the community. Now, here, he relates how the community will be sustained with life and power. In describing the union of the disciples with Jesus and the Father, he uses the metaphor of the vine which was a well known symbol from the Old Testament (Ps 80:8-19; Isa 5:1-7; Jer 2:21; Ezek 17:6-8, 19:10-14; Hos 10:1; Eccl 24:27). The word 'remain' or 'abide' occurs ten times in verses 1-11. This illustrates the mutual indwelling and continuous union with Jesus which becomes our life. If we refuse to take life from Jesus, the 'true vine', then we perish.

In Chapter 14 of John we read:

> Jesus replied, "Anyone who loves me will obey my teaching. My Father will love them, and we will come to them and make our home with them. Anyone who does not love me will not obey my teaching. These words you hear are not my own; they belong to the Father who sent me."
>
> (Jn 14:23f)

The Greek word for home is '*mone*', which is related to *menein*. Here Jesus is telling us that He and the Father live in us. They are closer to us than we are to ourselves. Teresa of Avila said we are God's Paradise. We have an infinite dignity. It is by love that the Father and the son indwell the person. It is by love they know us and we them. This union of love is achieved by the Holy Spirit, 'the Paraclete'.

"All this I have spoken while still with you. But the Advocate, the Holy Spirit, whom the Father will send in my name, will teach you all things and will remind you of everything I have said to you. Peace I leave with you; my peace I give you. I do not give to you as the world gives. Do not let your hearts be troubled and do not be afraid."

(Jn 14:25f)

The Holy Spirit accomplishes the work of indwelling. This fulfills the rebirth in the Spirit of 3:1-8. The Spirit will mediate Jesus' continuing presence in the community (14:15-17, 25-26; 15:26-27; 16:7-11, 12-15). It is by love that we fulfill the commandment of Jesus "Love one another as I have loved you" (Jn 13:34). Jesus promises not to leave us orphans because he will send the Holy Spirit to dwell with us. We come to know God by experiencing the intimacy of love that exists between the Father and the Son. By the Spirit we share in that intimacy:

"If you love me, keep my commands. And I will ask the Father, and he will give you another advocate to help you and be with you forever— the Spirit of truth. The world cannot accept him, because it neither sees him nor knows him. But you know him, for he lives with you and will be in you. I will not leave you as orphans; I will come to you. Before long, the world will not see me anymore, but you will see me. Because I live, you also will live. On that day you will realize that I am in my Father, and you are in me, and I am in you. Whoever has my commands and keeps them is the one who loves me. The one who loves me will be loved by my Father, and I too will love them and show myself to them."

(John 14:15-21)

Knowing Jesus is the same as knowing the Father since Jesus manifests him perfectly in his own person (Jn 14:8). He dwells in the Father and the Father in him. The divine empowerment Jesus experiences is available to us. We, his disciples, are called to manifest Jesus in the world. Love is the mode for knowing God, and Jesus and the Father will love and reveal themselves to those who love Jesus. We are promised the gift of the Spirit who is love to bring us into an intimate communion with Jesus and the Father. We live in God and he is us.

Jesus prays to the Father for his disciples:

> "They do not belong to the world, any more than I belong to the world. Consecrate them in the truth. As you sent me into the world, I have sent them into the world, and for their sake I consecrate myself so that they may be consecrated in truth."
>
> (John 17:16-19)

He prays that the disciples may be one as he and the Father are one. To consecrate them in the truth means he prays that they may be made holy by God's word (v.17) embodied in Jesus (1:9, 17; 8:31-32). My true home is with and in God. He says to all of us: "You are my Beloved, on you my favour rests" (Mk 1:11).

Living With Ambiguity:

In The Tablet (6 June, 2020, p.8f) A. N. Wilson discusses his new biography of Charles Dickens.[1] Dickens hated his mother. He was also cruel to his loyal wife. His was a divided personality. In the February edition of The Tablet, Maggie Ferguson wrote about the devastation brought to her by the posthumous revelations about Jean Vanier. It was discovered he was a sexual predator.

Dickens wrote about the centrality of Christian love in 'A Christmas Carol'. He wrote when many people had lost religious belief. Dickens' celebration of Christian love came as close as many Victorians felt to an acceptance of Christianity. As the stories of Dickens' home life began to unfold after his death there was a refusal to believe it. His daughter Katey wrote an autobiography which she later destroyed. She told of

---

[1] A. N. Wilson, They Mystery of Charles Dickens (London: 2020).

Dickens' double life, of his secret affair with the young actress, Nelly Ternon. Dickens was cruel to his wife at the same time.[2] Claire Tomalin shows this in her work.

The concept of the 'False Self' was introduced by Daniel Winnicott in 1960. The badly parented child has to create a compromise, has to learn to be a false self, in order to please his or her parents. This is usually unsuccessful. Such 'False Selves' often grow up to be cruel and controlling people, incapable of making their own parents or children happy. The hidden self is a wounded, unwanted, unloved child. In all of us there is a brokenness. The face we present to the world is the 'False Self'.

Henri Nouwen wrestled with the False Self and the feelings of being unloved and vulnerable. He shared his flaws in his books. He shared his vulnerability. It is in God we find acceptance, love and peace. We are called to make our 'home', our *'mone'* in him. Our negative image, our negative experiences tell us we are unlovable and that God cannot love us. Nouwen enables us to face our fears and allow ourselves to be loved.

He was influenced in his quest for God by people like Vincent Van Gogh and Rembrandt. Both of these were flawed human beings. Yet from the sufferings and mistakes of their lives they made beautiful art. Nouwen said that there are many tears in life but when he looks at Rembrandt or Van Gogh, their lives and their art consoles him more than anything else.[3] In their art we can see ourselves, our struggles and brokenness. We can come to face our fears and come to accept ourselves as we are. We are led to the presence of God. The Spirit is always at work calling us, broken as we are, into communion with God.

Nouwen had discovered a new place in him, the place "where God had chosen to live" and he was determined to live his life from that place. His writing points us to claiming our belovedness and not listen to the negative voices that are always with us. The spiritual life for him is a dynamic encounter with God.

[2] Claire Tomalin, The Invisible Woman (London: 1990).

[3] Henri Nouwen, Home Tonight (London: 2009) p. 13.

Self rejection is closely tied to our image of God. We need to meet him in the scriptures, in prayer. By healing our relationship with God, Nouwen helps us heal our relationships with ourselves. He meditates, as we will see, on Rembrandt's 'The Return of the Prodigal Son'. It is an icon to heal within us the image of the divine.

Wounds into Honours (Revelation of Divine Love, ch. 39):

This is an expression of Julian of Norwich. When we concentrate on ourselves and our weakness we feel discouraged, but in the hands of God "wounds are transformed into honours". This calls to mind what St. Paul said: "We know that all things work together for the good for those who love God, who are called according to his purpose" (Rom 8:28). St. Thérèse of Lisieux said that true sanctity consists in bearing with our faults patiently (LT 243, also M:C 2V°).

Henri Nouwen is somebody who suffered against his false self all his life. He was a Dutch Catholic priest, professor, writer and theologian. His interests were rooted in psychology and theology and how these related to spirituality, social justice and community. He taught at the universities of Notre Dame, Yale Divinity School and Harvard Divinity School. He was always seeking to find a place he would call 'home'. While he was at Yale he spent several months at the Abbey of the Genesee in the town of York, New York. He left Yale in 1981 and went to South America for six months. He taught at Harvard after this.

He was influenced by Jean Vanier, this was in a good sense because of what has been revealed of Vanier as a sexual predator. Henri went to live in the L'Arche Daybreak community in Richmond Hill, Ontario, Canada. He died in 1996.[4]

Nouwen came from a loving, caring family, but in his words:

[4] Many good biographies have been written about Nouwen; among them Jurgen Beumer, Henri Nouwen: A Restless Seeking for God (New York: 1997); Michael W. Higgins, Genius Born of Anguish (Mahwah, NJ: 2012); Michael Ford, Lonely Mystic: A New Portrait of Henri J. M. Nouwen (New York: 2018).

"Somehow fear of being rejected, of being abandoned, of being disliked has been with me as long as I can remember. I kept asking my parents, friends and colleagues in many different ways: 'Do you love me?' And I never heard a clear Yes that I could receive. I kept doubting, wondering, searching and begging for a final clear and total Yes, but it never seemed to come."

(First draft of The Prodigal Son)

Henri spent his life searching for the bonds of love that would satisfy his need for safety and belonging. "Do you love me?" was his final cry for love and affection. It was something that perplexed his parents, Maria and Laurent. This yearning for love, what he calls 'special love' (Home Tonight, xvii) was part and parcel of Henri's life. Many of his life decisions make sense in view of this dominant feature of his personality. It led him to join the priesthood and to a lifelong search and love affair with God. It also led to darkest night where loneliness and depression would overwhelm him.

His first book, *Intimacy*, was published in 1969 when he was thirty seven years old. In *Intimacy*, the search for love is equated with the search for home. In the Introduction, Nouwen says he will address "the seldom articulated and often unrecognised desire for a real home in the world" (p. 2). The word 'home' conjures up images of safety, rest and familial bonds. Home can be a place of unity, freedom and integration. Our true home is with God. This is something he developed in his work 'The Return of the Prodigal Son' (1992). In his later writings the answer to his lifelong search for love is found in God. In the Gospel of Mark we read: "You are my Son, the Beloved; with you I am well pleased" (Mk 1:11). This becomes central in his writings. We, all of us, are God's Beloved. We don't have to work to earn love; we are loved infinitely by God.

Henri was committed to his vow of celibacy. He wrote in 'Clowning in Rome':

"Celibacy, in its deepest sense of creating and protecting emptiness for God, is an essential part of all forms of

Christian life: marriage, friendship, single life, and community life… Every relationship carries within its centre a holy vacancy, a space that is for the first Love, God alone."

(Clowning in Rome, 43)

When Nouwen was ordained priest (1957) he asked his bishop could he study psychology. Nouwen studied as a Fellow in the Religion and Psychiatry Program at the Menninger Clinic in Topeka, Kansas. He became interested here in the Civl Rights Movement. In 1965 he travelled to the Southern United States to take part in the Selma to Montgomery marches.

Nouwen had been introduceed to the work of Anton Boisen by Willem Berger at the University of Nijmegen. Nouwen continued his work on Boisen when he moved to the United States to work at the Menninger Clinic.

Anton Boisen (+1965) graduated from Indiana University in 1897 and he taught French and German, first in high school and then later as a tutor at the university. During this period he suffered the first of several major psychotic episodes. He entered the Union Theological Seminary in the city of New York and graduated in 1911. He became a Presbyterian minister. Boisen worked with the YMCA in Europe during the First World War. When he returned from Europe he experienced another breakdown. He was plagued by mental illness all his life. He believed that some mental illnesses, such as schizophrenia, could be interpreted as one's attempts to solve the "problems of the soul". He sought to understand his mental illnesses and from this he wrote some of his best works.[5] Boisen founded the Clinical Pastoral Education (CPE) movement. Students were taught to think and reflect systematically about the human condition, both psychologically and theologically. A central tenet of Boisen's thought was that each person is a "living human document" on which the experiences of life are written. Think of the Scriptural passage from St. Paul: "You show that

---

[5] e.g. see Anton Boisen, The Exploration of the Inner World (New York: 1936).

you are a letter from Christ, the result of our ministry, written not with ink but with the Spirit of the living God, not on tablets of stone but on tablets of human hearts" (2 Cor 3:3). Boisen saw those being ministered to as living human beings and to focus our attention upon those who were grappling with the issues of spiritual life and death. Our own roundedness can help us ease something of the pain those we minister to are in. Nouwen uses his own life for his work. He shares thoughts and feelings, many of which most of us would like to hide. This helps him connect with the reader's experience. He learned this through Boisen and his case study method. He was moved by Boisen's autobiography 'Out of the Depths'.[6] Nouwen wrote: "What do these disturbances mean for me, a minister who is trained in the psychology of religion".[7] The idea of the 'Wounded Healer' comes from Carl Jung (+1961). He said those involved in psychoanalysis should be conscious of their own wounds. By dealing with and acknowledging our own woundedness we can hear what the other person is saying. Nouwen would develop these ideas and would write 'The Wounded Healer' in 1972.

Other major influences on Nouwen were Thomas Merton, Vincent Van Gogh and Rembrandt Van Rijn. We now join Nouwen in his search for the God of mercy and compassion and the search to find a home in him. Jesus said: "My Father's house has many rooms; if that were not so, would I have told you that I am going there to prepare a place for you" (Jn 14:2). The word used in Greek for 'many rooms', 'mansions' is the word we met *'mone'* [home]. We are called to this eternal home. Henri, in his writings, helps us make this journey.

[6] Anton Boisen, Out of the Depths: An Autobiographical Study of Mental Disorder and Religious Experience (New York: 1960).
[7] Henri Nouwen, Anton T. Boisen and Theology Through Living Human Documents, Pastoral Psychology 19, as 1st (September 1968) p. 50.

Chapter 2

The Wall:

I saw a model of anxiety on Pinterest. It was an iceberg. On the top above the water were things like negativity, over-planning, stress, a lack of focus and avoidance. However this was just the tip of the iceberg. Underneath was a whole mountain. The mountain was made up of many things, including being depressed, hurt, disrespected, feeling rejection and sadness, to mention but a few. Anxiety can follow on trauma. The effect of trauma overwhelms the brain's ability to cope. Feeling worthless, hurt and alone, the person in anxiety finds it difficult to cope. Loneliness, anxiety and what other people think of the anxious person is the lot of many. Soren Kierkegaard wrote from his experience of loneliness and anxiety.

Anxiety is the great enemy in the spiritual life. Our anxiety arises from a lack of love or, in the case of the trauma of abuse, a complete perversion of love. Children who are hurt do not hate the person who hurt or abused them, they turn inward and fall out of love with themselves. "Artists and poets strive to awaken the slumbering kernel of a better humanity, to inflame a love for higher things, to transform a common life into a higher one" (Schleiermacker).[1] Kierkegaard said:

> "Deep within every human being there still lives the anxiety over the possibility of being alone in the world, forgotten by God, overlooked among the millions and millions in this enormous household."
>
> (Journals and Papers 140; PAP. VIII1 A 363)

We acquire a sense of worthlessness from those who denigrate us. We feel threatened and every look or little event that touches our wound makes us withdraw more. Roger Waters of Pink Floyd used the image of a wall to show us how we lock ourselves into what we think is a

---

[1] Friedrich Schleiermacker, On Religion: Speeches to its Cultured Despisers, trans. Richard Crouter (Cambridge: 1996), p. 7.

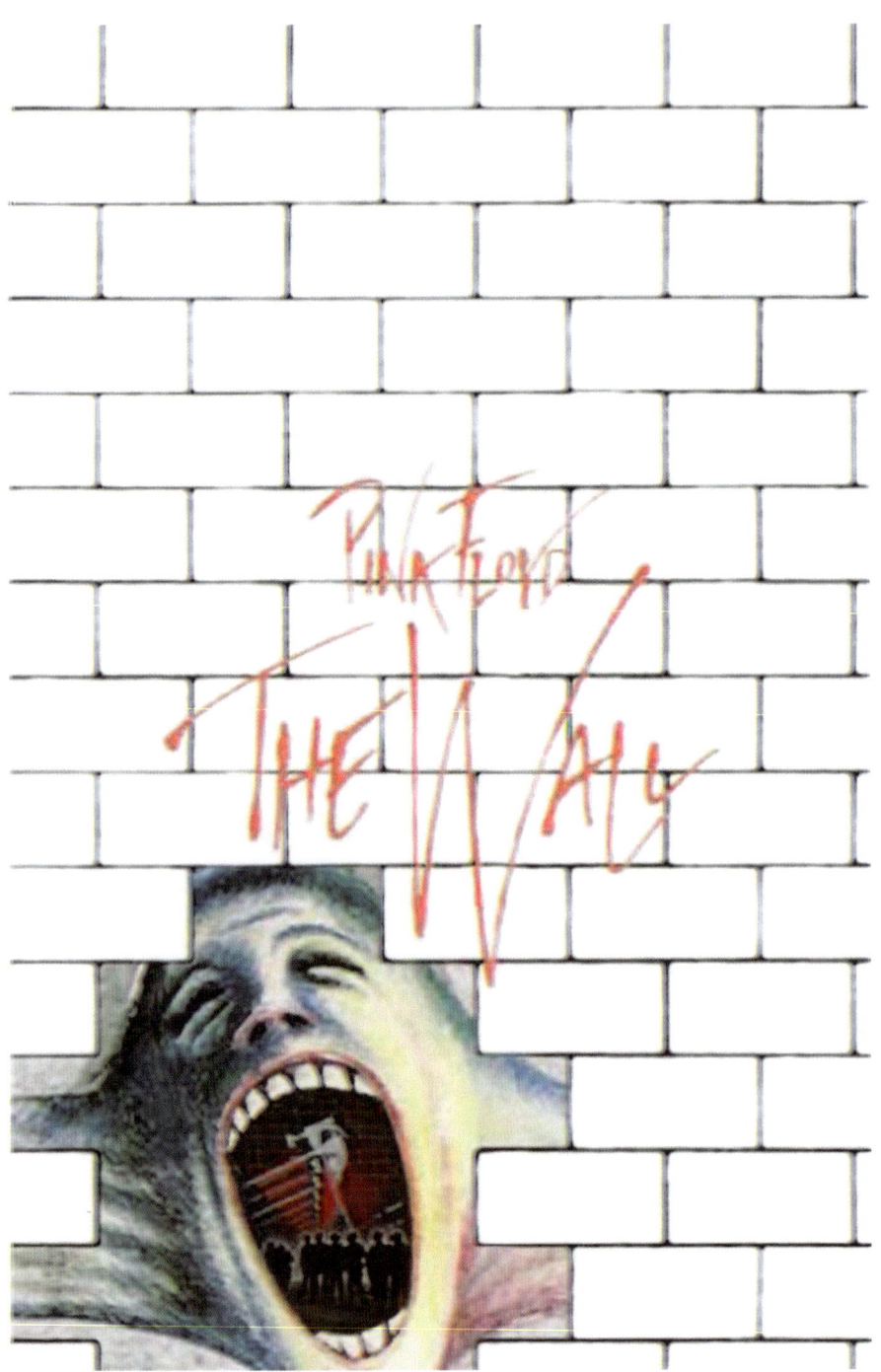

secure space where we can avoid reality and the world which can seem threatening. When we feel isolated we can think we are the only ones who feel this way. Kierkegaard reminds us:

> "Just as a physician might say there very likely is not one single living human being who is completely healthy, so anyone who really knows mankind might say that there is not one single living human being who does not despair a little, who does not secretly harbour an unrest, an inner strife, a disharmony, an anxiety about an unknown something or something he does not even dare to try to know, an anxiety about some possibility in existence or an anxiety about himself, so that, just as a physician speaks of carrying an illness in the body, he walks around carrying a sickness of spirit that signals its presence at rare intervals in and through an anxiety he cannot explain."[2]

One of the bands who looked at anxiety and loneliness is Pink Floyd in their album 'The Wall'. The idea of the Wall began in their 'In the Flesh Tour', in 1977. They played in large stadiums to big crowds. Roger Waters, the bassist with the group, disliked these mass gatherings. He preferred a more controlled and intimate relationship between the musicians and the audience. His dissatisfaction boiled over at the last show they played in Montreal's Olympic Stadium. Somebody let off firecrackers at the back and a group at the front made noise. Waters stopped playing and told the band to stop playing. He appealed for calm in the audience but they weren't listening. In a temper Waters spat at the audience. Waters said:

> "…there was one guy in the front row who was shouting and screaming through everything. In the end I called him over and when he got close enough I spat in his face. I shocked myself with that incident, enough to think, 'Hold on a minute. This is all wrong. I'm hating all this.' Then I began to think, what is it all about?"[3]

---

[2] Soren Kierkegaard, The Sickness unto Death (Princeton: 1983), p. 22.
[3] see Vernon Fitch, Pink Floyd: The Press Reports (Ontario: 2001).

Pink Floyd's producer saw Waters' distress and asked him to speak to a psychologist. Waters spoke of wanting to create a wall between himself and the audience. Thus the 'Wall' began to come into being.

'The Wall' tells the story of a character called 'Pink' who feels alienation because of the loss of his father and the traumatic interactions he has with authority figures. The song 'Another Brick in the Wall, Part 2' shows us the traumatic effects of being 'picked on' and bullied in school by a cruel teacher. Many from my generation can relate to this. I once met a former schoolfriend who was suffering from mental illness. He could not get over the trauma one particular teacher had caused him. Even though the events happened a long time ago, he still bore the mental scars many years later.

'Pink' – the hero of 'The Wall' – shuts himself away in a hotel room watching a war film. Pink remembers the death of his father in the Second World War, his upbringing by a protective mother and being shamed by a teacher (who in turn is humiliated by his wife). By the time he has become a teenager, Pink is pathologically agoraphobic and has constructed a wall around himself to shut himself off from the world. Eventually Pink suffers a new mental crisis. He trashes his room and shaves his head and body. He is given drugs to revive him and get him on stage. He transforms himself into a neo-nazi and leads the mobs in violence. He is arrested and thrown into prison. He is then judged at a court hearing in which his mother, his wife and his former teacher are called as witnesses. The verdict is eventually handed down:– Pink has to demolish the wall behind which he mistakenly thought he was safe. 'The Wall' became an album, a stage-show and a film directed by Alan Parker, starring Bob Geldof. The album was released in 1979. Roger Waters performed 'The Wall' in Berlin in 1990 (together with other musicians) to celebrate the fall of the Berlin Wall.

Waters hired Gerald Scarfe to do the artwork for 'The Wall'. Scarfe is an English cartoonist and illustrator. He has worked as cartoonist for The Sunday Times and illustrator for The New Yorker. Pink Floyd were attracted to Scarfe for some of his off-beat cartoons. In one such cartoon he showed Mickey Mouse smoking dope (not quite the Mickey Mouse that we had come to love).

Waters explained The Wall to Scarfe. He told him about the events of his father's death, his girlfriend's infidelity and his experience of bad teachers. Scarfe created a grotesque cast of characters that would go on to become iconic figures in the landscape of pop culture. Scarfe worked on the album, the stage-show and the 1982 film. One image that has stayed with me is that of children being pressed into a blender and they come out as spaghetti. It speaks to me of different times in my life. On a social level I hear people denigrating a broad education in areas such as history, art, religion and the humanities saying that children should concentrate more on maths. The Spaghetti machine image still holds. The song 'Another Brick in the Wall' comes in three parts. Part 1 shows Pink's sadness, Part 2 contains the line 'We don't need no education'. Waters is not against education but he is against the harsh regimes under which many suffered in the 1950's and 60's. He is pro- good education which equips the student for life and develops other talents. "We don't need no" is a double negative. In English grammar the second negative counters the first and the statement means: "We need education", that is, an education that develops our personality. 'Another Brick in the Wall, Part 3' shows Pink's anger at the world and his growing isolation. The songs about isolation and abandonment and the exploration of darkness and humanity makes The Wall a harrowing journey.

The song we will look at in depth, here, is: 'Another Brick in the Wall, Part 2'. It follows from the track: 'The Happiest Days of Our Lives'. This phrase describes fond memories of school days. Here the title is ironic because Pink's experiences were traumatic.

> "When we grew up and went to school
> There were certain teachers who would
> Hurt the children any way they could
> By pouring their derision
> Upon everything we did,
> And exposing every weakness,
> However carefully hidden by the kids."
> (The Happiest Days of Our Lives)

Cruelty was the order of the day for many children of that era. The children's weaknesses were exposed and the confidence of the child was often damaged. In the film based on The Wall, the teacher finds a book of Pink's poems on the desk, humiliates him in front of the rest of the students by mocking his ability. The teacher calls his poems "Absolute rubbish". This discouraging experience, in light of Andrew Brink's work 'Creativity as Repair', is a likely contributing factor to Pink's inability to accept his father's death. Brink says:

> "From the Romantic period of the eighteenth and early nineteenth centuries onward, the concept of imagination has increasingly been tied to the psychology of creativity. Developments in psychodynamic theory during the last few decades prompt a new attempt to be more precise about what imagination seeks to accomplish within the total psychological economy. I believe that its most important function is reconstructive in situations of loss of essential attachment figures, whether they be parents in early life or some combination of disruptions of the developmental process and later losses of sustaining personal relationships.... Every reader of literature, and of the biographies of writers, has noticed the high incidence of parent loss and forced adaptation among those who later become creative."[4]

Waters said his father was a school teacher who taught physical education and religious instruction. He was killed when Waters was three months old. "A wrenching waste. I concede that awful loss has colored much of my writing and my worldview."[5] By discouraging his writing of poetry, the teacher robs Pink of a powerful restorative activity and he becomes more withdrawn and locked into himself. According to Waters, many of his teachers just tried to keep the children quiet and crush them into the proper shape for going to university and doing well.[6]

[4] Andrew Brink, Creativity as Repair (Hamilton, ON: 1982).
[5] Timothy White, "Pink Floyd" Penthouse (September 1988) p. 158 - 166.
[6] Interview with Tony Vance, 1979 (November 30, BBC Radio 1).

The image of "crushing" people into the right shape is symbolically represented throughout the film by hammers, one of the abiding symbols of The Wall. The teacher is in turn victimised at home.

> "But in the town, it was well known,
> When they got home at night, their fat and
> Psychopathic wives would thrash them
> Within inches of their lives."

Then a loud shriek rings out and we enter "Another Brick in the Wall, Part 2". This song would be released as a single and become a worldwide hit. It begins:

> "We don't need no education.
> We don't need no thought control.
> No dark sarcasm in the classroom,
> Teachers leave them kids alone.
> Hey! – teacher! leave them kids alone."

The "dark sarcasm" in the classroom was devastating for the young and undermined their self-confidence. Waters saw education and, by extension, other groups as a "factory farm technique" to produce a docile and unquestioning workforce. The children are marched mechanically through a maze and on a conveyor belt where they disappear behind a brick wall. They reappear on the other side of the wall sitting at their desks and are now wearing the pink masks that rob them of their identities. Eventually the kids rebel and burn down the school. This revolt only took place in Pink's imagination. Back in the classroom, he still feels lonely and alienated. He sees the teacher as being just another "brick in the wall":

> "All in all it's just another brick in the wall
> All in all you're just another brick in the wall."

The whole experience plays a major role in forming Pink's obsessive personality. He begins to feed back into the world what he received.

Helen Cecil Sherrill made the following remarks:

> "Miller speaks of the pattern of the abused child, masochistically trying to please the oppressor, futilely trying to gain acceptance. Finally, losing all hope, he polarizes in the manner of enantiodromia from the masochist into the sadist. The child's rage merges with the introjected cruelty of the adults who victimize him, and the vicious cycle is perpetuated."[7]

Later, when Pink takes on the personality of a neo-nazi he repeats the abusive behaviour he has learned and unleashes violence on others. This is a nightmare scenario.

Breaking a Wall:

The "Wall" ends with a call to tear down the Wall. This is to risk vulnerability and the possibility of being hurt again. Henri Nouwen wrote a book called "Life of the Beloved".[8] When Henri was at Yale Divinity School he was interviewed for the Connecticut section of the Sunday edition of The New York Times by Fred Bratman. Henri couldn't help noticing that the young man was ill at ease with himself – so he engaged him in conversation. Fred felt stymied by his job and really wanted to write seriously. He could not really express himself in a short article of about 750 words. Henri sensed a beautiful heart in his friend, a heart that wanted to give and create. Fred was close to abandoning his dreams. Henri said:

> "By now I had become angry at him, at society and, to some degree, at myself for letting things just be as they are. I felt a strong urge to break down all these walls of fear, convention, social expectations and self-deprecation, and I

---

[7] Helen Cecil Sherrill, The Quality of Childhood Consciousness and its Significance, PhD thesis, Emory University, 1991.

[8] Henri Nouwen, Life of the Beloved (London: 2016 ed.).

blurted out, 'Why don't you quit your job and write your novel?' 'I can't,' he said ... I kept pushing him, 'If you really want it, you can do it. You don't have to be the victim of time and money.'"

(Life of the Beloved, p. 15)

Eventually the young man did leave his job and with Henri's help explored writing his novel and other avenues for self-expression. Fred was Jewish and he laid down a challenge in turn for Henri. He asked him to write for those like him trapped in so many ways in New York. Henri wondered at first what could he say but eventually he wrote "Life of the Beloved". He had torn down Fred's wall and now he reached out to others.

The Beloved:

Nouwen learned of the beloved when he read the story of Jesus coming out from the water after his baptism: "No sooner had Jesus come up out of the water than he saw the heavens torn apart and the Spirit, like a dove, descending on him. And a voice came from Heaven: 'You are my Son, the beloved; my favour rests on you'." (Mk 1:10f). The scene that Mark portrays shows that Creation is happening again. In Genesis 1, God's Spirit hovers over the waters. In Jewish writings of Mark's time, the heavens are opened "to pour out the Spirit as a blessing of the heavenly Father" (The Testament of Judah). Here God's Spirit descends like a dove, a term used of the beloved in the Song of Songs. This idea becomes explicit when the "voice from the heavens" says: "You are my beloved Son". St. Paul tells us:

> "For those who are led by the Spirit of God are the children of God. The Spirit you received does not make you slaves, so that you live in fear again; rather the Spirit you received brought about your adoption to sonship. And by him we cry, "Abba, Father." The Spirit himself testifies with our spirit that we are God's children."

(Rom 8:14-16)

The Spirit that believers experience is the foretaste, the first fruits, the downpayment of what is to come. We are "the children of God", sons and daughters of God, brothers and sisters of Jesus. The Holy Spirit has brought about this adoption as children.

The Holy Spirit dwells in all people and it is in this light that Nouwen speaks. He sees all of humanity as being "beloved of God".

Nouwen points out that it is certainly not easy to hear that we are the beloved of God. Our world, like the world of Pink, is filled with voices that shout: "You are no good, you are ugly, you are worthless; you are despicable, you are nobody – unless you can demonstrate the opposite" (Life of the Beloved, p. 30). Nouwen tells us that these negative voices are loud and persistent. Many of us can relate to that. He goes on to say that over the years he has come to realise that the greatest trap in our lives is not success, popularity or power but self-rejection. He is surprised at how constantly and quickly he gives in to the temptation of self-rejection.

> "As soon as someone accuses me or criticises me, as soon as I am rejected, left alone or abandoned, I find myself thinking: 'Well, that proves once again that I am a nobody.' Instead of taking a critical look at the circumstances or trying to understand my own and others' limitations, I tend to blame myself – not just for what I did, but for who I am. My dark side says: 'I am no good ... I deserve to be pushed aside, forgotten, rejected and abandoned.'"

Even when we see someone proud and arrogant we find this is just another way of dealing with the feelings of worthlessness. Both self-rejection and arrogance pull us out of the common reality of existence. Beneath arrogance there lies much self-doubt. Whether I am inflated or deflated I have lost touch with the truth of who I am and my vision of reality is distorted. Self-rejection is the enemy of the spiritual life because it rejects the sacred voice that calls us the 'Beloved'. Being the Beloved of God expresses the core truth of our existence (p. 33).

Henri tells us how hard it was for him to hear that voice telling us that we, too, with Jesus are the 'Beloved'. He listened more to other voices that said: "Prove you are worth something: do something relevant, spectacular or powerful, and then you will earn the love you so desire" (p. 33).

Nouwen alludes to 1 Kings 19. Here Elijah retires to the mountain of Horeb waiting for the Lord to come. We read:

> "Then a great and powerful wind tore the mountains apart and shattered the rocks before the Lord, but the Lord was not in the wind. After the wind there was an earthquake, but the Lord was not in the earthquake. After the earthquake came a fire, but the Lord was not in the fire. And after the fire came a gentle whisper. When Elijah heard it, he pulled his cloak over his face and went out and stood at the mouth of the cave."
>
> (1 Kings 19:11-13)

The queen Jezebel is trying to kill Elijah. Elijah runs away. Here at Horeb – the place to which he has retreated – God will 'pass by'. What happens next are powerful displays of nature: a strong wind, an earthquake and then fire. But Elijah does not recognise God in these forces. They are followed by a "light silent sound" (a more literal translation) and in the gentle silence Elijah recognises that God is present.

That gentle silence is all around us and if we have ears to hear it tells us, each one of us: "You are my Beloved". Jesus came and died to teach us this truth. There is a constant fight in us as there was in Nouwen. All the signs of love we get are not sufficient to convince us we are 'Beloved'. We are like Pink withdrawn behind our walls. Yet that "gentle silence" will not be silenced. Nouwen tells us:

> "Well, you and I don't have to kill ourselves. We are the Beloved. We are intimately loved long before our parents, teachers, spouses, children and friends loved or wounded us. That's the truth of our lives. That's the truth I want you

to claim for yourself. That's the truth spoken by the voice that says, 'You are my Beloved.'"

(Life of the Beloved)

In the Book of Isaiah we read: "Do not fear, for I have redeemed you: I have summoned you by name: you are mine" (Isa 43:10). In Psalm 139:13-14 we read: "For you created my inmost being; you knit me together in my mother's womb. I praise you because I am fearfully and wonderfully made; your works are wonderful". God's care for each of us is as tender as a mother for her children (Isa 49:15). He says: "See I have engraved you on the palm of my hand" (Isa 49:16) and "Before I was born the Lord called me: from my mother's womb he has spoken my name". This is the source of the spiritual journey Nouwen's friend Fred – and those who listen – are making. We have to let the gentle silent voice, "You are my Beloved" gradually take root in us and live from that place, not giving heed to the voices that tell us we are no-good. Being the Beloved is the origin and fulfillment of the life of the Spirit (p. 43). Psychologists speak about changing "the pictures in your head". The voices that tell us we are useless create their own images and patterns. The voice that tells us "You are Beloved" changes this. We begin to change the images we have of ourselves and of others. Henri uses four words – 'taken'; 'blessed'; 'broken' and 'given' – to explain the movement of the Spirit within us. We should always remind ourselves "I am the chosen child of God" when the world tells us otherwise.

1. Taken:

Henri addresses Fred and his wife Robin telling them that they are chosen by God. They reminded him that though the Jewish people were 'chosen' there is still a lot of anti-semitism around. They have positive and negative associations with the word 'chosen'. Fred's ancestors suffered much before they came to the United States.

Being God's chosen means we all have been seen by God from all eternity and everyone is seen as a unique, special and precious being. "You are precious and honoured in my sight and I have loved you" (Isa 43:4). These words are spoken by the prophet Isaiah in the name of God. In Jeremiah we read: "Before I formed you in the womb I knew you" (Jer 1:5). The eyes of love which are God's, see us as of infinite beauty; as of eternal value.

In our competitive world, the fact that we are chosen does not mean that others are rejected. In life there is much competition in so many areas and when we do not succeed we feel down. God loves each of us individually. The mystics teach us that God loves each individual so much that one would think he or she was the only person in the world. All people are created and accepted in their uniqueness.

Nouwen points out that this is something we have to grow into. Many people have had traumatic childhoods or traumatic experiences in later life and have suffered much abuse and rejection. One such person was Ella Fitzgerald. She was abused as a child, ran away from her care home and lived rough on the streets. Yet when she sang, she was full of joy. She was not overcome by her past. Others who do not feel loved by those who gave them life can suffer from a low self-esteem that can easily lead to depression, despair and even suicide. The great spiritual battle begins – and never ends – with reclaiming the truth of our being chosen.

To battle the negative voices of our world we have to see that much of our society is manipulative, controlling, power hungry and destructive. We have to face this and in the face of rejection remind ourselves we are the chosen of God – even if for a while we do not feel this. The next step is to seek places and people where our truth is spoken and where we are reminded of our deepest identity as God's chosen. We have to learn to listen to the men and women throughout our history and the history of the world who, through their lives and their words, call us back to our true identity. Paul Tillich described faith as "the courage to accept acceptance". We have to make a leap of faith to embrace God's view of us, not the negative voices that afflict us. Nouwen then tells us we have to add gratitude. We 'are' because God has chosen us. When we can be grateful, this can spread to our lives. We begin to notice more the good things and the good people around us. We begin to replace the negative voices with those that are more positive. Nouwen describes a girl called Helen who came to the Daybreak community. This is where people with disabilities who are vulnerable people. She was very withdrawn and 'odd'. Henri was a little frightened of her, but he still reached out to her. Gradually she came out of herself and her smile lit up the whole community and house. Henri said:

> "When we keep claiming the light, we will find ourselves becoming more and more radiant. What fascinates me so much is that every time we decide to be grateful it will be easier to see new things to be grateful for. Gratitude begets gratitude, just as love begets love."
>
> (p. 61f)

Henri had to affirm his own goodness before he could affirm Helen's goodness. Then he could reach out to Helen and love saw her blossom.

In his book "Following Jesus",[9] he writes about acknowledging our pain and bringing it to Jesus who is one with us. We find we are not alone. He says:

> "Or we pray, 'Lord, I am so fearful today. I don't know where it comes from, but I am anxious and fearful. It is there. Lord, I want to bring it into your presence and bring it right into the Garden of Gethsemane and connect it with your anguish so that my fear becomes your struggle. The struggle to live.'"

My experience of rejection is united with Christ's experience.

When we struggle with something great or small this allows us, slowly, to 'come home to ourselve's and 'be with God'. Jesus reveals God's love to us and by the power of the Holy Spirit God dwells in us. Our true home is there with them. In uniting all our struggles with Jesus we grow to become the person we are called to be. People like Ss. Francis of

---

[9] Henri Nouwen, Following Jesus: Finding Our Way Home in an Age of Anxiety (London: 2019).

Assisi, Teresa of Avila and John of the Cross speak about compassion. They speak about the mystery of suffering with Christ. They look upon the One who is pierced and broken and they see the love of God radiating on them. We can join him and 'feel the love'. We can bring our whole being into God's presence and my cross can merge with that of Jesus.

2. Blessed:

As Beloved children of God we are blessed. Henri remembers the time Fred took him to a Bar Mitzvah. The young man read from the Book of Genesis (Life of the Beloved, p. 67) and gave a short sermon. He was affirmed by the Rabbi and blessed by his parents. His father said: "Son, whatever will happen to you in your life, whether you will have success or not, become important or not, will be healthy or not, always remember how much your mother and I love you". Henri was very moved. He says: "What a grace such a blessing is".

Henri became increasingly aware of how much we "fearful, anxious, insecure human beings are in need of a blessing. Children need to be blessed by their parents and parents by their children. We all need each others' blessing" (p. 68). There are many people who have had adverse childhood and later life experiences. We have already seen 'Pink'. Many have suffered emotional, physical and sexual abuse. They may have witnessed domestic violence and felt powerless. They may have been neglected as children. They do not feel worthy of a blessing. They turn the rejection they received inward and reject themselves.

Henri tells us, then, what he means by blessing. In Latin the word "to bless" is *benedicere*. It is made up of two parts which mean literally: speaking (*dicere*) and well (*bene*) or saying good things of someone. It affirms the person before God. It means to say yes to a person's belovedness. A blessing draws on the goodness of God within and touches the goodness of the other and calls forth his or her Belovedness.

Henri discovered the power of blessing in the L'Arche Daybreak community. A girl called Janet, a member with a disability, came to Henri and asked for a blessing. He responded in an automatic way by tracing with his thumb the sign of the cross on her forehead. Janet protested that she wanted a 'real blessing'. He told Janet he would bless her after the prayer service. Then after the meeting Janet came up to him, put her arms around him and put her head against his chest. He said "Janet, I want you to know you are God's Beloved daughter. You are precious in God's eyes. Your beautiful smile, your kindness to the people in your house and all the good things you do show us what a beautiful being you are. I know you feel a little low these days and that there is some sadness in your heart, but I want you to remember you are a very special person, deeply loved by God and all the people who are here with you" (p. 70). Then many more members with disabilities came forward. Then some of the assistants came forward. To one of the assistants he said: "John, it is so good that you are here. You are God's Beloved son. Your presence is a joy for us all. When things are hard and life is burdensome, always remember you are loved with an everlasting love" (p. 71). John welled up with tears in his eyes, thanking Henri.

We all need to hear we belong to a loving God who always loves us. Abraham and Sarah, Isaac and Rebecca, Jacob, Leah and Rachel, they all received that blessing and so became the fathers and the mothers of our faith. We need to hear that voice which says to us "You are my beloved child, on you my favour rests". We can become easy victims of our manipulative world, but that gentle voice within us reminds us we are loved. When I read Henri's words I remember all the lack of affirmation I experienced in life and I can be more aware of being cursed rather than blessed. I have to come away and listen for that voice again.

In 'Following Jesus' Henri tells us that when we pray, we connect our whole life with God's life. God's love can flow through our veins. We can live our struggles in a different way. One time he was very depressed. He was in Flagstaff, Arizona, so he decided to go to the Grand Canyon. Looking at the Grand Canyon – at that enormous abyss of beauty – the strange depression began to fall away. He felt the silence. The image of the Grand Canyon stayed with Henri for a long time. God is like the Grand Canyon. God suffered the wound, the wound of all humanity and Henri felt that if he could enter into the presence of that wound, his own wound became a light burden or a light pain. He found he could live his pain and not be destroyed by it. He could acknowledge his pain and not be paralyzed by it. The Grand Canyon invited him to enter an abyss of Divine Love and to experience the fact that he is immensely loved and cared for. He was invited to enter life with a new heart, with God's heart. His very breath would be the breath of the Holy Spirit.

St. Augustine said that "our hearts are restless and they will not rest until they rest in God" (Confessions 1:1). In each of us there is an infinite longing for love that can only be satisfied by the Love of God. We drift away and seek that love in other places that cannot fill our need. We have to regain a proper sense of ourselves and receive God's blessing, his affirmation that we are truly loved. This is when we truly become ourselves and return to right relationship with God and each other. The real 'work' of prayer is to become silent and listen to the voice that 'speaks well' of us. We find it hard to enter that silence, but when we do, the Holy Spirit – who is very gentle and hidden – teaches us we are 'Beloved'. We can sense that we are in the Presence of God by the work of the Holy Spirit. The Father loves the Son, and the Son loves the Father. The Holy Spirit can be seen as the 'embrace' of the Son and Father. We are called into that embrace. St. Bernard also speaks of the Holy Spirit as being the kiss of God. It is God teaching us with his loving kiss. Whatever image we use, God communicates to us that we are loved. We are called – in our turn – to bring that blessing to others. There are so many like 'Pink' that have received only rejection. The power of love can help them and we can mediate God's love to them.

3. Broken:

When Fred and Henri met, both were broken and in becoming friends they supported each other. Henri supported Fred through a painful separation and divorce. Fred helped Henri through a long period of depression. The most-celebrated musical compositions, the most-rated paintings and the most-read books are often direct expressions of the human awareness of brokenness.

The leaders and prophets of Israel, who were clearly chosen and blessed, all lived very broken lives. We share a common 'chosen, blessed and broken' humanity with them. Henri is convinced that every human being suffers in a way no other human beings suffer. There can be a resemblance but each person is unique. Our brokenness is truly ours. There is much suffering in society but Henri becomes increasingly aware that on a day-to-day basis the most common and hardest is that of a broken heart. St. Teresa of Calcutta said the great pain of our world is loneliness. People are not valued in their uniqueness. Many feel the pain of being rejected, ignored, despised and left alone. In the L'Arche community there were many people with severe disabilities. The hardest part of life for them could often be the feelings of being useless, worthless, unappreciated and unloved. When we feel we are of no value to anyone, we can lose our grip on life.

Our sexuality reveals to us our enormous yearning for communion. Henri discovered late in life that he was gay and he sought to integrate this into his personality. His gay friends hoped he would write on this and that this would give them courage as gay Christians. It was something Henri did not achieve. Henri saw society as being fragmented, family life being sundered by physical and emotional distance. There was no place for him to feel at home. He often longed for a healing touch or a reassuring embrace. He says the fragmentation and commercialisation of our world make it hard to find a place where our whole being – body, mind and heart – can feel safe and protected. He was very aware of the suffering caused by AIDS.

Henri says the way to respond to our brokenness is to face it squarely and acknowledge it honestly. He reminds Fred of the pain he was in when he realised his marriage was over and how he grew through this experience. Leonard Cohen said: "There is a crack in everything, that's how the light gets in" (Anthem) and Oscar Wilde said: "How else but through a broken heart may Lord Christ enter in" (The Ballad of Reading Gaol).

Henri, himself, experienced a time of deep depression. He had a friendship with a worker at L'Arche but he was very needy and the friendship didn't work out. He came to realise the deep truth that our human suffering need not be an obstacle to the joy and peace we desire but can become, instead, the means to it.

The second response to our brokenness is to place it under the blessing. We see our suffering as a curse and feel we are no good. Our call is to place our brokenness in the light of blessing. What seemed intolerable, now becomes a challenge. Henri saw his experience of his dependence on the affection and friendship of one person as an expression of his need for total surrender to the living God, the only one who could satisfy the desire of his heart. He had to learn this through his experience of depression. None of the reality of our brokenness disappears when we follow Henri's way but the One who calls us the Beloved can make our brokenness shine like a diamond.

He recalls with Fred the time they went to the Lincoln Centre and heard Leonard Bernstein conducting music by Tchaikovsky. Bernstein had introduced Henri to the joy of music. As a teenager he had been to one of Bernstein's concerts in Holland and was very moved by this experience. When 'West Side Story' appeared on screen, Henri fell in love with the songs and would return when he could to see the film again and again.

As he writes about Brokenness, he recalls a scene from Bernstein's 'Mass' in honour of the late John F. Kennedy. Towards the end of the work, the priest is lifted up by his people. He towers high above them carrying in his hands a glass chalice. Suddenly, the human pyramid collapses and the priest comes tumbling down. The glass chalice falls to the ground and is shattered. As he walks through the debris of his former glory children's voices are heard: "Praise, praise, praise". Suddenly the priest notices the broken chalice. He says: "I never realised that broken glass could shine so brightly". Gerard Manley Hopkins says:

> "I am all at once what Christ is,
> since he was what I am, and
> This Jack, joke, poor potsherd,
> patch, matchwood, immortal diamond,
> Is immortal diamond."
>
> (That Nature is a Heraclitean Fire and
> the comfort of the Resurrection)

For Hopkins, the resurrection counters the darkness of our state. Christ was "as I am" but we are called in our brokenness to come to new life in Christ. We are 'immortal diamond'. We are under the blessing.

4. Given:

In the trial scene in The Wall, Pink sees images of his past life. The crime with which he was initially charged was: "showing feelings of an almost human nature" – which he did throughout the work by withdrawing into himself to protect himself. The crime with which he is, ultimately, charged and for which he is punished, is that of not having expressed his feelings. Because he did this others around him suffered. Pink's deepest fear was exposing his fragility and sensitivity. The wall has to come down. He has to risk being human. The last words in The Wall are:

> "All alone, or in twos,
> The ones who really love you
> Walk up and down outside the wall.
> Some hand in hand,
> Some gathering together in bands.
> The bleeding hearts and the artists
> Make their stand.
> And when they've given you their all,
> Some stagger and fall, after all it's not easy
> Banging your heart against some mad bugger's
> Wall."

There are people who love us and we have to take the risk of reaching out. Henri found that in his life that he expected too much from his relationships. He felt an infinite need for love which can only be filled with God.

Henri spoke to his friend Fred about how he found love with Robin. After the failure of his first marriage and his disappointment with his life-choice he was aware of his brokenness but he still reached out again. He changed his life choice and married Robin. His wounds were turned into blessings. Henri said one of our greatest joys is to give. We can give love and acceptance to those around us. We become beautiful people when we give whatever we can give, a smile, a handshake, a kiss, an embrace, a word of love, a present, a part of our life (Life of the Beloved, p. 106). A happy life is a life for others. That truth is usually discovered when we are confronted by our weakness. Our real gift is not so much what we can do, but who we are.

Henri draws some examples from the community at Daybreak. One is Linda who has a speech impediment. She has a unique gift for welcoming people. Many who stayed in Daybreak remember Linda because she made them feel at home. Another example is Adam, who is unable to speak, walk or eat without help. He has the great gift of bringing peace to those who care for him. The visible brokenness of these people with disabilities allows them to offer their gifts freely and without inhibition.

Henri then goes on to meditate on death. In our society we run away from death. We do not even get time to grieve. We do not allow ourselves. Yet for those who accepted death Henri found they left a memory behind. They sowed seeds of hope in those who remembered them. He uses the example of Francis of Assisi who died in 1226. His spirit lives on. His death was a true gift and nearly eight centuries after his death he fills those touched by him with great energy and life. He goes on bearing new fruit around the world. His spirit keeps descending on us (Life of the Beloved, p. 120). St. Thérèse of Lisieux said: "After my death I will let fall a shower of roses; I wish to spend by heaven in doing good works upon the earth".[10] She wanted to be "prayer before the face of God" (see Ps 108:3). Many cures have been attributed to her, including that of Edith Piaf, who had a lifelong devotion to her. Thérèse became known as the healer of the 20th century.

Henri went to live in Lima in Peru at one stage in his life. He was in a hurry and he had many plans. On his way he met a group of children

---

[10] Jean LaFrance, When You Pray, Say: "Father" (Sherbrooke, Q C: 2000) p. 146.

who came over to him and would not let him go. Eventually he stayed with the children. They did not want his great plans but they valued his company. It was more important to be present to them than to be preoccupied with his great plans. In giving himself to the company of the children he experienced a great joy. It is God who saves the world. We can be his partners in whatever way he calls us.

The Wall (conclusion):

The conclusion of the film 'The Wall' shows young children in an area where there has been rioting. For a moment we can think that the whole cycle of building a wall starts over again. There is an image of hope suddenly. A young boy finds a Molotov cocktail from which he removes the rag and then he empties the liquid from the bottle. He has no wish to do violence to another person. There is hope.

Chapter 3

Rembrandt:
The Return of the Prodigal Son

Simon Schama says of Rembrandt:

> For Rembrandt as for Shakespeare, all the world was indeed
> a stage, and he knew in exhaustive detail the tactics of its
> performance: the strutting and mincing; the wardrobe and
> the face paint; the full repertoire of gesture and grimace; the
> flutter of hands and the roll of the eyes; the belly laugh and
> the half-stifled sob. He knew what it looked like to seduce,
> to intimidate, to wheedle, and to console; to strike a pose or
> preach a sermon; to shake a fist or uncover a breast; how to
> sin and how to atone; how to commit murder and how to
> commit suicide. No artist had ever been so fascinated by the
> fashioning of personae, beginning with his own. No painter
> ever looked with such unsparing intelligence or such
> bottomless compassion at our entrances and our exits and
> the whole rowdy show in between.[1]

'Visio Divina' (divine seeing) is an ancient contemplative practice that
invites the practitioner to encounter the divine through images. It shares
its origins with Lectio Divina, the practice of reading Scripture and then
holding what one has read in his or her heart and contemplating it from
there. Visio is an interaction with an image to create an experience of the
Spirit. We come to experience what all the characters feel. "Gazing",
Nouwen explains, "is probably the best word to touch the core of
Eastern spirituality. Whereas St. Benedict, who has set the tone for the
spirituality of the West, calls us first to listen, the Byzantine fathers
focus on gazing".[2] This describes Nouwen's interaction with
Rembrandt's "The Return of the Prodigal Son".

[1] Simon Schama, Rembrandt's Eyes (New York: 1999), p. 8.
[2] Henri Nouwen, Behold the Beauty of the Lord: Praying with Icons (Notre Dame: 1987), p. 22.

Rembrandt Van Rijn (1660 - 1669):

He was born in Leiden in the Dutch Republic, now the Netherlands. Religion became a central theme in Rembrand's paintings. His mother was a Roman Catholic and his father belonged to the Dutch Reformed Church.

At the age of 14, he enrolled in the University of Leiden. He preferred art and was soon apprenticed to Pieter Lastman. He opened an art studio in Leiden. In 1629 Rembrandt was discovered by the statesman Constantijn Huygens who commissioned important works and introduced him to Prince Frederik Hendrik who purchased his works.

Rembrandt moved to Amsterdam. He made a lot of money and spent a lot. The self portraits painted during this time reveal Rembrandt as a man hungry for fame and adulation. However, this short period of success was followed by much grief, misfortune and disaster. After having lost his son Rumbartus in 1635, his first daughter Cornelia died in 1638 and his second daughter, also named Cornelia, died in 1640. Then he lost his wife, Saskia, who died in 1642. Rembrandt had one son left, Titus. After Saskia's death Rembrandt had an unhappy relationship with Titus' nurse, Geertje Dircx, ending in a lawsuit and the confinement of Geertje in an asylum. This was followed by a more stable relationship with Hendrickje Stoffels. She bore him a sone who died in 1652 and a daughter, Cornelia, the only child who would survive him.

During these later years Rembrandt's popularity plummeted. His financial situation worsened and in 1656 Rembrandt was declared insolvent. All of Rembrandt's possessions, his own works, his house in Amsterdam and everything in it, were sold. He was never fully free of debt. He began to regard "men and nature with an even more penetrating eye, no longer distracted by outward splendour or theatrical display".[3] More pain is to follow. In 1663 Hendrickje dies and five years later he sees not only the marriage, but also the death of his beloved son, Titus. Only his daughter, Cornelia, his daughter-in-law Magdalene Van Loo, and his granddaughter Titia survived him.

[3] Jacob Rosenberg, Rembrandt: Life and Work, 3rd edition (London: 1968), p. 26.

Vincent Van Gogh saw Rembrandt's painting of the "Raising of Lazarus" and some of the other later works of Rembrandt. He remarked that the man who painted these paintings must have died a thousand deaths. Rembrandt did not fall into despair but created works of great depth and pathos. It is interesting to read different biographies of Rembrandt. Some paint him as getting what he deserved, emphasizing the wrong turns he made. Others see him as a great human being.[4] The truth is that he was a mixture of both. We have to live with ambiguity. If Rembrandt wasn't a flawed human being with great struggles then he would not have given the world such great beauty.

Henri Nouwen, in the Autumn of 1983, was at the L'Arche community in Trosly in France. One day he went to visit a friend, Simone Landrien, in the community's documentation centre. As they spoke, his eyes fell on a large poster on her door. He saw a man in a great red cloak tenderly touching the shoulders of a disheveled boy kneeling before him. He could not take his eyes away. He saw the intimacy between the two figures, the golden yellow of the boy's tunic and the mysterious light, engulfing them both. Most of all, it was the old man's hands which touched the boy's shoulder that touched him deeply. The poster was a reproduction of Rembrandt's Prodigal Son. He gazed on the poster.

Nouwen was invited by friends Bobby Massie and his wife, Dana Roberts, to join them on a trip to the Soviet Union. He had the opportunity to visit the 'Hermitage' in St. Petersburg. The painting of the 'Prodigal Son' was acquired by Catherine the Great in 1766. Henri had the opportunity to see the real painting. Due to the kindness of the Hermitage staff he spent hours 'gazing' on the painting and imagining the different characters Rembrandt painted. This gazing would ultimately lead to his work "The Return of the Prodigal Son: A Story of Homecoming" (New York: 1992).

---

[4] e.g. Gary Schwartz, Rembrant: zign Leve, zign Schilderijen (Maarssen, 1984) and Charles L. Mee, Rembrandt's Portrait: A Biography (New York: 1988). These are the works cited by Nouwen in The Return of the Prodigal Son: A Story of Homecoming (New York: 1992), p. 65.

The Road to the 'Prodigal Son':

Before he would write about his experience of seeing the painting he had a journey to undergo. He came to the L'Arche community at Daybreak in 1986 leaving his teaching and university career behind. While at Daybreak, Nouwen was paired with Adam Arnett, a 'core member' of the community. Adam had profound disabilities and Henri had to look after him. "It is I, not Adam, who gets the main benefit from our friendship", Nouwen said.[5] He wrote about his relationship with Arnett in a book entitled "Adam: God's Beloved" (New York: 1997).

A couple of years after arriving Nouwen explained part of his attraction to the L'Arche way of life:

> L'Arche has its own unique tone. It's not an institution. It's not a group home. It's a spiritual community where handicapped people are in the center. L'Arche exists not to help the mentally handicapped get "normal", but to help them share their spiritual gifts with the world. The poor of spirit are given to us for our conversion. In their poverty, the mentally handicapped reveal God to us and hold us close to the Gospel. That's a vision we have to nurture and deepen. I'm just beginning to discover it. I'm no expert on it. Nobody really is. But we live it very tenderly.[6]

In other ways Daybreak was more difficult than he expected. He, after his university career, was like a fish out of water. He shared a house with several core members. People with handicaps were called core members. He had to help with meals, household chores, dressing and feeding the core members and other routine daily tasks.

A great trial came to Nouwen. He was friendly with Nathan Ball whom he had originally met in Trosly. Their friendship was renewed at

---

[5] see Philip Yancey, 'Holy Suffering', Christianity Today, vol. 40, no. 14 (9 December 1996), p. 60.

[6] Arthur Boers, 'L'Arche and the Heart of God' in The Road to Peace: Writing on Peace and Justice by Henri Nouwen (New York: 1988) 151-9.

Daybreak. It had been life giving at the start but Nouwen became obsessed with the friendship. Ball began to feel claustrophobic and cut off all contact between them. Nouwen descended into a deep depression. Nouwen left the community for a while to get professional help. Reflecting back on this time in his life Nouwen said:

> "Being among the handicapped people, I discovered my own handicaps, particularly with regard to issues of affection and friendship. As I lived longer in the Daybreak community old demons around my need for affection revisited me and I began to find it difficult to love freely without being selfish and demanding" (Home Tonight, 8).

Nouwen moved to 'Homes for Growth' in Winnipeg, Manitoba, a spiritual community and retreat centre that offered therapeutic services for clergy.

> "The anguish completely paralyzed me," wrote Nouwen in 'The Inner Voice of Love', the published diary of this episode in his life. "I could no longer sleep. I cried uncontrollably for hours. I could not be reached by consoling words or arguments.... All had become darkness. Within me there was one long scream coming from a place I didn't know existed, a place full of demons".[7]

Nouwen began to recover. One day Joe Egan wrote to him reminding him he was much loved at Daybreak and every day they prayed for him. "You must remind yourself you are much loved by the people of Daybreak".[8]

Sue Mosteller played a key role in Nouwen's restoration to health. She belonged to the Sisters of St. Joseph, Toronto. She mentored and

---

[7] Henri Nouwen, The Inner Voice of Love: Journey Through Anguish to Freedom (New York: 1986), XIV.
[8] Joe Egan, Letter to Henri Nouwen, January 1, 1988.

challenged Nouwen, aways acknowledging his gifts. He entered a healthy friendship with Nathan Ball and found relative peace.

In 1989 Nouwen was struck by the outside rearview mirror of a van and had to undergo surgery for the removal of his spleen in hospital. In a subsequent paperback 'Beyond the Mirror'[9] he spoke of how his accident brought him close to death and a new experience of God. Henri was treated with dignity and respect by strangers and that made him feel safe.

> "I do not have many conscious memories of being so completely cared for and, at the same time, of being taken so seriously. Perhaps it was this that filled me with such a profound sense of security."
>
> (Beyond the Mirror, p. 29)

As he tried to cope with the possibility of death he had an experience of pure and unconditional love, an intensely personal presence that asked him to trust.

> "It was not a warm light, a rainbow, or an open door that I saw but a human yet divine presence that I felt, inviting me to come closer and to let go of all fears."
>
> (Beyond the Mirror, p. 33)

He felt he had been called to live eternity while still exploring the human search in time. He now knew at timeless realm where there is unconditional love and acceptance. After being critically injured he told his father, who had flown from Holland with his sister Laurien to be with him, that he loved him and was grateful to receive his love. He spoke of many things that he had not spoken of before. Nouwen explained this encounter as a "spiritual event" that allowed him to "return from a false dependence on a human father who cannot give me all I need to a true dependence on the divine Father" (Prodigal Son, 78).

Henri always wanted his father's approval but never felt he could get it. Now there was a reconciliation.

---

[9] Henri Nouwen, Beyond the Mirror (London: 1990).

Nouwen was, as we saw, influenced by Anton Boisen. He visited Boisen in August 1964. His insights from the visit foreshadowed those of the 'Prodigal Son'.

> "When I left I was very thankful that I had had the opportunity to meet this man whose suffering had become a source of creativity. The condition in which I found him showed clearly that his basic suffering never completely left him."[10]

Boisen was very ill. He had suffered another breakdown. Henri saw how Boisen's sufferings led to his creativity and to his insights. His suffering was a source. He saw that Boisen's sufferings never totally left him. Henri felt that his own sufferings allowed him to be sensitive to the many forms of human suffering. Both Henri and Boisen struggled with fear related to scrupulousness. Yet our wounds can become a deep source of beauty. Boisen gave Nouwen a model for radical vulnerability. He taught Nouwen to be courageous with his weaknesses. By sharing them he would be a source of healing for himself and others. In the 'Prodigal Son' Nouwen used his own life as the basis for his book.

Nouwen was touched by the Spirit by all these encounters. He felt the love of God poured into his heart "by the Holy Spirit given us" (Romams 5:5). Nouwen speaks of the Holy Spirit in this way.[11] He speaks about those people who have died in our life. They still have a place in our hearts and keep nurturing us. This is a great mystery. It is a mystery Jesus reveals to us in the most fulsome way. He says "It is good for you that I am going, because if I do not leave I cannot send you my Spirit. When I leave I will send you my Spirit and my Spirit will lead you to the full truth" (John 16:7). The word "truth" means a full relationship with God. The Spirit will lead us into union with God and only by leaving us can this take place. Jesus dies and rises again. Then after his ascension the Spirit can lead us into the most intimate

---

[10] Boisen in the Henri J. M. Archives and Research Collection, Box 7, File 01-2.

[11] Henri J. M. Nouwen, Following Jesus: Finding our Home in an Age of Anxiety (London: 2019).

communion with God. In the Spirit God is with us in an intimate and personal way. He is closer to us than we are to ourselves. God lives in us. He is the one who suffers with us. The very breath we take comes from the Spirit of God. He is the Lord and giver of life. We breathe the Spirit of God. By the Spirit God dwells in the heart of our being. Under the guidance of the Spirit the first disciples began to understand Jesus' message. They realised they could live an interior life, a life in Christ. St. Paul said: "I have been crucified with Christ and I no longer live, but Christ lives in me. The life I now live in the body, I live by faith in the Son of God, who loved me and gave himself for me" (Gal 2:20). Jesus is so intimately with us that we are one. We breathe with the breath of his Spirit. We are called to manifest that Spirit to the world.

The Return of the Prodigal Son:

The parable of the Prodigal Son is found in the Gospel of Luke. It reads:

> Jesus continued: "There was a man who had two sons. The younger one said to his father, 'Father, give me my share of the estate.' So he divided his property between them.
> "Not long after that, the younger son got together all he had, set off for a distant country and there squandered his wealth in wild living. After he had spent everything, there was a severe famine in that whole country, and he began to be in need. So he went and hired himself out to a citizen of that country, who sent him to his fields to feed pigs. He longed to fill his stomach with the pods that the pigs were eating, but no one gave him anything.
> "When he came to his senses, he said, 'How many of my father's hired servants have food to spare, and here I am starving to death! I will set out and go back to my father and say to him: Father, I have sinned against heaven and against you. I am no longer worthy to be called your son; make me like one of your hired servants.' So he got up and went to his father.

"But while he was still a long way off, his father saw him and was filled with compassion for him; he ran to his son, threw his arms around him and kissed him.

"The son said to him, 'Father, I have sinned against heaven and against you. I am no longer worthy to be called your son.'

"But the father said to his servants, 'Quick! Bring the best robe and put it on him. Put a ring on his finger and sandals on his feet. Bring the fattened calf and kill it. Let's have a feast and celebrate. For this son of mine was dead and is alive again; he was lost and is found.' So they began to celebrate.

"Meanwhile, the older son was in the field. When he came near the house, he heard music and dancing. So he called one of the servants and asked him what was going on. 'Your brother has come,' he replied, 'and your father has killed the fattened calf because he has him back safe and sound.'

"The older brother became angry and refused to go in. So his father went out and pleaded with him. But he answered his father, 'Look! All these years I've been slaving for you and never disobeyed your orders. Yet you never gave me even a young goat so I could celebrate with my friends. But when this son of yours who has squandered your property with prostitutes comes home, you kill the fattened calf for him!'

"'My son,' the father said, 'you are always with me, and everything I have is yours. But we had to celebrate and be glad, because this brother of yours was dead and is alive again; he was lost and is found.'"

(Luke 15:11-32)

At this point in the Gospel Jesus is journeying towards Jerusalem. He deals with the restoration and forgiveness of the sinner. In the parable of the Prodigal Son, according to ancient Jewish custom (see Num 27:8-11; 36:7-9) an inheritance is the father's property. He chose to give this property to his sons. The son is asking his father for a part of the Father's life. It is as if he, the father, were dead. The Father has patience and grants the son his desire. The young son squanders his money. He feeds pigs, which represents everything reprehensible to Jewish sensibility. The son repents and comes home. The Father welcomes him. The parable then switches to the older son who is upset at the way the younger son has been welcomed. The father insists that the prodigal is both a son to him and a brother to his other son. The elder son is upset but the father goes on loving him too. As with all parables we are asked where do we fit in the parable.

Rembrandt painted the scene giving it his own interpretation and this invites us to enter the scene. This is what Henri did and he produced the book "The Return of the Prodigal Son: A Story of Homecoming". Simon Schama says of Rembrandt:

> Rembrandt liked this. From the beginning, he was powerfully drawn to ruin; the poetry of imperfection. He enjoyed tracing the marks left by the bite of worldly experience: the pits and pocks, the red-rimmed eyes and scabby skin which gave the human countenance a mottled richness. The piebald, the scrofulous, the stained, and the encrusted were matters for close and loving inspection; irregularities to run through his fingering gaze. Other than the Holy Scripture, he cared for no book as well as the book of decay, its truths written in the furrows scored on the brows of old men and women; in the sagging timbers of decrepit barns; in the lichenous masonry of derelict buildings; in the mangy fur of a valetudinarian lion. And he was a compulsive peeler, itching to open the casing of things and people, to winkle out the content packed within. He like to toy with the poignant discrepancies between outsides and insides, the brittle husk and the vulnerable core.
>
> (Rembrandt's Eyes, p. 13)

The painting Schama alludes to is "The Artist in his Studio". Rembrandt is not afraid to show the real state of his studio in which his art is forged. "All these materials, he [Rembrandt] translated faithfully into pain, and

The Artist in his Studio c.1628

did so with such intense scrutiny and devotion that the patch of crumbling fabric begins to take on a necrotic quality like damaged flesh. Above the door another veinous crack is making swift progress through the plaster" (Schama, ibid). Rembrandt shows us the deep emotions that lie beneath in our vulnerable centre.

In his painting of the Prodigal Son the Father appears to be blind. He communicates by touch. The prodigal is turned away from us. He is buried in the bosom of his forgiving father. He is broken in his journey from transgression to atonement. The soles of he's feet are lacerated and pierced. His finery hangs in pathetic rags. The father, mantled in red, his face shining with consummate peace, places his hands on the boy's shoulders. It is a form of resurrection, a transformation of death into life. The elder son is seen scowling in the corner. The father tells him in the Gospel account "He, your brother, was dead and is now alive". We see the younger son kneel against the loins of his father, eyes shut, arms

51

The Return of the Prodigal Son   c.1669

across his chest. "They melt together into a single form, the pathetic shred of humanity returned to the boundlessly encompassing compassion of his creator" (Rembrandt's Eyes, 685).

Rembrandt painted 'Simeon in the Temple with the Christ Child' (see Luke 2:25-38) around the same time as 'The Return of the Prodigal Son'. Both these events take place in St. Luke's Gospel. Luke is the

Simeon with the infant Christ Child in the Temple   c.1669

patron saint of doctors and healers. In the two paintings neither man has his eyes open, but they rather deliver and receive the balm of grace with their eyes closed. Simeon cradles in his arms the Christ child. Simeon is irradiated by an invisible light, the light of grace, the light of the Spirit. Rembrandt leads us into the healing vision of St. Luke.

We now share Henri's reflections on the Prodigal son. He uses both Visio divine and Lectio divine. He gazes at the painting and we with him – *Visio*. He also meditates on the words of the Gospel – *Lectio*.

The Return of the Prodigal son: Part 1, The Younger Son:

Henri speaks about Rembrandt's two later paintings 'The Return of the Prodigal Son' and 'Simeon with the Child Jesus'. Both Simeon and the father of the returning son carry within themselves that mysterious light by which they know things. This inner light had remained hidden for a long time for Rembrandt. Only gradually and after much anguish did he come to know that light within himself and then in those he painted. Rembrandt was for a long time the young man "who left for a distant country where he squandered his money" (Luke 15:13). As a young man Rembrandt had all the characteristics of the prodigal son: brash, self-confident, spendthrift, sensual and very arrogant. His main concern was making money. However this short period of success, popularity and wealth was followed by much grief, misfortune and disaster. As Nouwen looks at the repentant son in the painting and then moves his eyes to the compassionate father he sees that the glittering lights reflecting from golden chains, harnesses, helmets, candles and hidden lamps have died out and are now replaced by an inner light. "It is the movement from the glory that seduces one into an ever greater search for wealth and popularity to the glory that is hidden in the human soul and surpasses death" (p. 33). The full title of Rembrandt's painting is "The Return of the Prodigal son". Implicit in the "return" is a leaving. The father who welcomes the son back is overjoyed because this son "was dead and has come back to life: he was lost and is found" (Lk 15:24). The son in the painting is dressed in rags that betray the great misery he is in. The son, before he left, had said to his father "Let me have the share of the estate that will come to me" (Lk 15:12). The evangelist Luke tells us this story so simply that it is difficult to realise what this statement means. Kenneth Bailey, in his explanation of Luke's story, shows that the son's manner of leaving is tantamount to wishing that his father were dead. Bailey writes:

> "For over fifteen years I have been asking people of all walks of life from Morocco to India and from Turkey to the Sudan about the implications of a son's request for his inheritance while the father is still living. The answer has always been emphatically the same ... the conversation runs as follows:
> Has anyone ever made such a request in your village?
> Never!
> Could anyone ever make such a request?
> Impossible!
> If anyone ever did, what would happen?
> His father would beat him, of course!
> Why?
> The request means – hew wants his father to die."[12]

The implication is that the son is saying his father is as good as dead to him. When Luke writes that the son went off to a far country (Lk 15:13), he speaks about a drastic cutting loose from the way of living, thinking and acting that has been handed down through the generations. The distant or far country is the world in which everything considered good and holy at home is disregarded.

This parable expresses the boundlessness of God's compassionate love. Nouwen says when he places himself "in the story under the light of that divine love, it becomes painfully clear that leaving home is much closer to my spiritual experience than I might have thought." (p. 37)

The father's touching the son is an everlasting blessing: the son resting against his father's breast is an "eternal peace". Christian Tümpel

---

[12] Kenneth E. Bailey, Poet and Peasant and Through Peasant Eyes: A Literary-Cultural Approach to the Parables in Luke (Grand Rapids, Mich: 1983), p. 161f.

writes: "The moment of receiving and forgiving in the stillness of its composition lasts without end. The movement of the father and the son speaks of something that passes not, but lasts forever."[13] Jakob Rosenberg summarises what we see and read beautifully when he writes: "The group of father and son is outwardly almost motionless, but inwardly all the more moved ... the story deals not with the human love of an earthly father ... what is meant and represented here is the divine love and mercy in its power to transform death into life."[14]

Leaving home is a denial of the spiritual reality that we belong to God. God holds me in an eternal embrace, I am indeed "carved in the palms of God's hands" and hidden in their shadows (Isa 49:16). Leaving home means ignoring the truth that God has "fashioned me in secret, moulded me in the depths of the earth and knitted me together in my mother's womb" (Ps 139:13-16). Leaving home is living as if I had no home and I look for "home" in places that cannot be "home". I go from disaster to disaster and am not happy.

Home is the centre of my being where I can hear the voice that says: "You are my Beloved, on you my favour rests" (Mk 1:11). This voice spoke often to Henri in the past and continued to address him. When he recognises he is the "Beloved" he is free to live and give life.

Henri goes on to ponder on the times he has left "home". He became deaf to the voice that called him the "Beloved". Seeing the touch of the blessing hands in the painting, really God's hands, and hearing the voice calling him the Beloved are one and the same. In the tenderness of God's voice was touch and touch was voice (p. 40).

There are other voices. These voices say, "Go out and prove you are something." Soon after Jesus heard the voice calling him the Beloved he was led by the Spirit into the desert to battle the other voices that

---

[13] Christian Tümpel (with a contribution by Astrid Tümpel) Rembrandt (Amsterdam: 1986), p. 350, translated by Henri Nouwen.

[14] Jakob Rosenberg, Rembrandt: Life and Work, 3rd edition (London and New York: 1968), p. 231, 234.

demanded his attention. These voices say I am not going to be loved without my having earned it through determined efforts and hard work. They want me to prove to myself that I am worth being loved and they push me to do everything in my power to get acceptance from those around me. They blind me to the fact that love is a totally free gift. These are the voices we pick up as we go through life. Those who have suffered abuse or violent rejection or bullying are affected by these voices and the voice that says we are Beloved seems far away. These voices lead us into the "distant country". Henri tells us he constantly falls back into the same trap listening to the negative voices. "I find myself wondering why someone hurt me, rejected me, or didn't pay attention to me. Without realizing it, I find myself brooding about someone else's success, my own loneliness, and the way the world abuses me" (p. 41). All these voices show him how fragile his faith is that he is God's Beloved. He is afraid of being "disliked, blamed, put aside, passed over, ignored". As he hears these voices he finds he is living in a distant, far country.

The world seems to say "Yes, I will love you if you are good-looking, intelligent and wealthy. I love you if you have a good education, a good job and good connections. I will love you if you produce much and buy much." There are many "ifs" in the world's love. Those who become ill, physically or especially mentally, are treated with disdain. There are many elderly in nursing homes who never receive visitors. There are many in hospitals who are left alone by those who should look after them. We are not allowed to grieve. Get back to work – you have to move on.

"Addiction" may be the best word that explains the lostness of our world. Our addictions make us cling to what the world proclaims as the keys to self-fulfillment: accumulation of wealth and power; attainment of status and admiration; lavish consumption of food and drink, and sexual gratification without distinguishing between lust and love (p. 43). We find ourselves in the far distant country. when Nouwen looks at Rembrandt's painting he sees the end of a great rebellion. The son leaves the far country and finds his father's hands are always stretched out in love and blessing. He is always there to embrace us. In this is our home and our healing. We all crave love and affection. We crave to be accepted. These cravings are often denied and we seek for this love anywhere. We do not hear the voice calling us Beloved. The prophet Elijah waits on Mount Horeb for God to pass by:

> The Lord said, "Go out and stand on the mountain in the presence of the Lord, for the Lord is about to pass by."
> Then a great and powerful wind tore the mountains apart and shattered the rocks before the Lord, but the Lord was not in the wind. After the wind there was an earthquake, but the Lord was not in the earthquake. After the earthquake came a fire, but the Lord was not in the fire. And after the fire came a gentle whisper. When Elijah heard it, he pulled his cloak over his face and went out and stood at the mouth of the cave.
> (1 Kings 19:11-13 [NIV version])

I can allow the loud, powerful voices take over my life. They lead me into depression and despondency. I need to be still like Elijah on Mount Horeb and hear the gentle whisper "You are my Beloved". This is the key to finding a home for my heart in God.

The young man held and blessed is a poor man. Rembrandt shows this. His head is shaven. The head is that of a prisoner where hair had been shaved off. The clothes Rembrandt gives him barely cover his body. The yellow-brown, torn undergarments just cover his exhausted, worn out body from which all strength is gone. This is a man dispossessed of everything except for a short sword hanging from his hips. This is the badge of nobility. We see in him emptiness, humiliation and defeat. Nouwen says that the further he lives away from the place where God dwells, the less he hears the voice calling him the Beloved. When he does this he tries to please, to achieve success, to be recognised. He craves for acceptance and becomes jealous of those he perceives as having more than him. He loses his inner peace.

The younger son could only work at feeding pigs. This image would not be lost on Jesus' Jewish audience. He was truly lost and it was this complete loneliness that brought him to his senses. He still remains his father's child. He returns to his father. He says: "I no longer deserve to be called your son, treat me as one of your hired men." (Luke 15:19). When the father saw him he was "filled with compassion for him; he ran to his son, threw his arms around him and kissed him" (Luke 15:20). This is the moment Rembrandt captures. It looked as if the son had to lose everything before he could really become the son of his father.

Henri, himself, felt like someone who had lost everything. He recalls his obsessive relationship with Nathan Ball and his breakdown. He explains how he was always tempted to wallow in his lostness. This happened over and over again when he said to himself: "I am no good. I am useless. I am worthless. I am unlovable. I am a nobody." (p. 50). He had countless events and situations in which he had to convince himself his life was worth living. These passages speak to the hurt many of us feel. Abuse, bullying make people feel this way. Many people in our world pick up these messages that they are no good, useless, worthless and unlovable. Many spent lives in trying to compensate for this pain they feel.

As he tries to come back to that centre where God lives, he wonders will he be welcome. He feels intensely his failures and thinks he will be rejected. He clings to his sense of worthlessness, but God's love is greater than our failings. He has to come again and again to that place and hear the voice of love telling him and all of us, "You are my Beloved". One of the great challenges of the spiritual life is to receive God's forgiveness which is his gift. When we do this we allow him to do the healing, restoring and renewing of spirit. Jesus makes it clear that the way to God is the same as the way to a new childhood: "Unless you turn and become like little children you will never enter the Kingdom of Heaven." (Matt 18:13).

Once Nouwen was studying a print of 'The Return of the Prodigal Son' which he showed to a group of friends and was interested in what they thought. One of them, a young woman, stood up and looked at the head of the younger son. She said: "This is the head of a baby who has just come out of his mother's womb. Look, it is still wet, and the face is still fetus-like." (p. 54). Nouwen wondered was Rembrandt painting not just the return to the Father, but also the return to the womb of God who is Mother as well as Father? We do not know if this is so but we can use it for our meditation on the painting. The younger son is made new and we can take his place in being renewed.

The word 'prodigal' means being wastefully extravagant. Jesus was 'prodigal' in this sense. He gave of himself for others and when he returned to the Father he brought broken humanity with him. Nouwen quotes Frère Pierre Marie who speaks of Christ in the following words:

> He, who is born not from human stock, or human desire or human will, but from God himself, one day took to himself everything that was under his footstool and he left with his inheritance, his title of Son, and the whole ransom price. He left for a far country … the faraway land … where he became as human beings are and emptied himself. His own people did not accept him and his first bed was a bed of straw! Like a root in arid ground, he grew up before us, he was despised, the lowest of men, before whom one covers his face. Very soon, he came to know exile, hostility, loneliness … After having given away everything in a life of bounty, his worth, his peace, his light, his truth, his life … all the treasures of knowledge and wisdom and the hidden mystery kept secret for endless ages; after having lost himself among the lost children of the house of Israel, spending his time with the sick (and not with the well-to-do), with the sinners (and not with the just), and even with the prostitutes to whom he promised entrance into the Kingdom of his Father; after having been treated as a glutton and a drunkard, as a friend of tax collectors and sinners, as a Samaritan, a possessed, a blasphemer; after having offered everything, even his body and his blood; after having felt deeply in himself sadness, anguish, and a troubled soul; after having gone to the bottom of despair, with which he voluntarily dressed himself as being abandoned by his Father far away from the source of living water, he cried out from the cross on which he was nailed: "I am thirsty." He was laid to rest in the dust and the shadow of death. And there, on the third day, he rose up from the depths of hell to

where he had descended, burdened with the crimes of us all, he bore our sins, our sorrows he carried. Standing straight, he cried out: "Yes, I am ascending to my Father, and your Father, to my God, and your God." And he reascended to heaven. Then in the silence, looking at his Son and all his children, since his Son had become all in all, the Father said to his servants, "Quick! Bring out the best robe and put it on him; put a ring on his finger and sandals on his feet; let us eat and celebrate! Because my children who, as you know, were dead have returned to life; they were lost and have been found again! My prodigal Son has brought them all back." They all began to have a feast dressed in their long robes, washed white in the blood of the Lamb.[15]

The light that surrounds the father and the son speaks of the glory that awaits the children of God. It calls to mind the majestic words of John: "… we are already God's children, but what we shall be in the future has not yet been revealed. We are well aware that when he appears we shall be like him, because we shall see him as he really is" (1 John 3:2).

There are other characters in Rembrandt's picture. They seem indifferent and don't seem to be affected by what has happened. They add a restraining note to the painting and prevent any notions of a quick, romantic solution to the question of reconciliation. We must continue to grow everyday. There is another character who is positively hostile. He is the elder son and we now turn to him.

The Return of the Prodigal Son: Part II, the Elder Son:

In Luke's parable the elder son was out in the field when the younger son came home. When he returns home the welcome party is in full flow. Barbara Joan Haeger showed that the parable of the Prodigal Son and the parable of the Pharisee and the tax collector were closely linked

---

[15] Frère Pierre Marie, Les fils prodigues et le fils prodigue, Sources Vives, Communion de Jerusalem, Paris (March 1987), p. 87-93. Translated by Henri J. M. Nouwen.

(p. 63).[16] The seated man beats his breast representing the sinners and tax collectors, while the man standing represents the Pharisees and scribes (Luke 18:9-14). Rembrandt puts the elder son as the most prominent witness. Haeger says Rembrandt holds on "not to the letter but to the spirit of the biblical text" (p. 173). Rembrandt showed his own spiritual battle in the painting. He invites us to consider ours. This is true to the way Jesus spoke the parable.

The elder son is also part of Rembrandt's experience. Gary Schwartz describes Rembrandt as "a bitter, revengeful person who used all permissible and impermissible weapons to attack those who came in his way."[17] He badly treated Geertje Direx, with whom he had lived for six years. He conspired to have her locked up in an asylum and he made certain when there was talk of her being released he blocked her release. During the year 1649, when many tragedies dogged Rembrandt, he emerges as a man lost in bitterness and a desire for revenge. He has one of the characteristics of the elder son.

In the painting the elder son looks with disdain at the scene. The light on the face of the elder son is cold and restricted. He was the one who worked hard every day and fulfilled all his obligations. He is a resentful, bitter, angry young man. Nouwen saw himself in the elder son. He worked hard to get acceptance from people like his father and authority figures, but he longed to run away from this way of life. The elder son says: "All these years I have slaved for you and never once disobeyed any orders of yours, yet you never offered me so much as a kid for me to celebrate with my friends" (Luke 15:28). In this complaint, obedience and duty have become a burden, and service has become slavery.

The 'lostness' of the younger son is obvious. He rebelled against morality and allowed himself to be swept away by his own lust and greed. The lostness of the elder son is harder to gauge. When he is confronted by his father's joy at the return of his brother, a dark power

---

[16] Barbara Joan Haeger, The religious significance of Rembrandt's Return of the prodigal son: an examination of the picture in the context of the visual and iconographic tradition, PhD thesis (Ann Arbor, Mich: University of Michigan Microfilms International, 1983), p. 173.

[17] Gary Schwartz, op. cit., p. 65 (translated by Henri Nouwen).

erupts in him and boils to the surface. Suddenly, there becomes glaringly visible a resentful, proud, unkind, selfish person (p. 71). Henri looks into himself and the lives of the other people and he sees how much damage resentment can do to the person. There is much judgment of others, condemnations and prejudice among the 'saints'. There is much frozen anger among people who say they do not want 'to sin'. All this resentment makes it difficult to feel at home in the Father's house.

At the heart of the elder son is a complaint that cries out: "I tried so hard, worked so long, did so much and I have not received what others get so easily. Why do people not thank me, not invite me, not play with me, not honour me, while they pay so much attention to those who take life so easily and so casually?" (p. 72). Henri remembers how much he would catch himself complaining about little rejections, little impolitenesses, little negligences. He would find himself grumbling, lamenting and griping. This would take his joy away. In the painting the elder brother stays out in the dark. He cannot enter the Father's light. The interpretation of the elder son's reaction is left to the viewer. Jesus did not provide an end to the story. That has to be supplied by us in our lives. When we gaze at the painting we see ourselves reflected in the different characters. Whether I am the younger son or the elder son, God's only desire is to bring me home. Arthur Freeman writes:

> "The father loves each son and gives each the freedom to be what he can, but he cannot give them freedom they will not take nor adequately understand. The father seems to realise, beyond the customs of his society, the need of his sons to be themselves. But he also knows their need for his love and a "home". How their stories will be completed is up to them. The fact that the parable is not completed makes it certain that the father's love is not dependent upon an appropriate completion of the story. The father's love is only dependent on himself and remains part of his character. As Shakespeare says in one of his sonnets: 'Love is not love which alters when it alteration finds.'"[18]

---

[18] Here Henri quotes from Arthur Freeman, "The Parable of the Prodigal", unpublished manuscript.

The father pleads with the elder son, "My son, you are with me always and all I have is yours" (Luke 15:31). The Greek word used for 'son' is *teknon* which is an affectionate form of address. He tells his son "you are with me always". He indicates here that his love embraces the elder son. Nouwen quotes the Gospel of John: "In the house of my father there are many places to live" (Jn 14:2).

Each child of God has his or her unique place, all of them in God. Here we can let go of all comparison, all rivalry and competition and surrender to the Father's love. I have to learn to trust and surrender to that love.

Along with trust there must come gratitude, the opposite of resentment. I can choose to stand in the darkness like the elder brother or come into the father's embrace. There is an old Estonian proverb that says: "Who does not thank for little will not thank for much". Jesus reveals to us that we are God's beloved. There is no distance, fear or suspicion between Jesus and the Father. In the Holy Spirit we can enter that space and feel the embrace of the Father's love. Nouwen describes how he made peace with his father and entered a new, loving relationship. This happened after his accident when his father came to visit him when he was at death's door (p. 83).

The Return of the Prodigal Son: Part III, The Father:

Sue Mosteller wrote to Henri when he was undergoing therapy in 1987. She spoke about his reflections on the two sons. She asked him to think about what it would mean for him to identify with the Father. She wrote:

> But I have also been asking myself who the Father is. You describe Him so well It is obvious that He is our Father, God. But perhaps there is something else here to think about yourself.
>
> As I see you over these past years and months I ask myself if the real call for you is the call to become the Father. Once the sons have made their unique passages are they not then ready to become like the Father, to become the Father? And truly Henri, aren't you right there? Is that what this passage

is all about? Isn't this why you chose to come to Daybreak in the first place; because in your life journey you were more ready to be Father and you knew somewhere in yourself that it was time to "put away the things of the son"?

I can see this call for your rising up from within yourself, the call to become Father. Isn't your heart burning within you to be able to love others as that Father loves? Wouldn't you find a deep sense of fulfillment to be able to be here in this community as the Father was in his own home? Here you would be in your home and you would wait patiently for the errant ones to come home and you would accept and hold onto the resentful ones until they were ready to make their own passage. Does this make any sense to you?[19]

This letter touched Henri. He began to meditate on the father in Rembrandt's painting. He began to see in the father a human expression of divine compassion. The parable could be called the parable of the 'Compassionate Father'. Every detail of the father's figure – his facial expression, his posture, the colour of his dress and the still gesture of his hands – speaks of love, a love for humanity that existed from the beginning and ever will be (p. 93).

Here everything comes together: Rembrandt's story, humanity's story and God's story. Time and eternity intersect. Nouwen sees in the father in the painting infinite compassion, unconditional love and everlasting forgiveness. These are divine realities. Here both the human and the divine, the fragile and the powerful, the old and the eternally young are fully expressed. This is Rembrandt's genius (ibid). The spiritual truth is shown in the flesh. Paul Baudiquey writes: "The spiritual in Rembrandt... pulls its strongest and most pleasant accents from the flesh".[20]

Baudiquey says that Rembrandt's vocation was to grow old (Rembrandt, ibid). Rembrandt had always painted old people. After his trials at home and at work, he became interested in blind people. He is attracted to

[19] see Gabrielle Earnshaw, Henri Nouwen and the Return of the Prodigal Son: The Making of a Spiritual Classic (Brewster, Massachusetts: 2020) p. 79f.
[20] Paul Baudiquey, La Vie et l'Oeuvre de Rembrandt (Paris: 1984), p. 9.

Tobit and the near blind Simeon. He paints them many times. As Rembrandt grew old he became more in touch with the immense beauty of the interior life. In his innermost being he discovers the light that comes from an inner fire that never dies, the fire of love, the fire of the Holy Spirit. He transforms the visible to show the fire of love that lives in him. The father cannot make his sons love him. He lets them be free to find their own way. This causes him great pain and loneliness, the loneliness of God who sees us hurt each other in so many ways. There is no lust, greed, anger, resentment, jealousy or vengeance in his children that has not caused him grief. From the deep place of love in his heart, he reaches out to heal and restore his children. This is what Rembrandt shows us in the painting. He painted from a heart that knew many tragedies and he paints with compassion.

In the painting the two hands of the father are different. The father's left hand touching the son's shoulder is strong and muscular. The right hand is refined, soft and very tender. It lies gently on the son's shoulder. The feminine right hand is similar to the hand of 'The Jewish Bride' painted in the same period (p. 99).

The Jewish Bride

Rembrandt represents the God in whom both manhood and womanhood, fatherhood and motherhood, are fully present. The gentle, caressing hand echoes the words of the prophet Isaiah "Can a woman forget the baby at the breast, feel no pity for the child she had borne? Even if these were to forget, I shall not forget you. Look, I have engraved you on the palms of my hands" (Isa 49:15-16).

Then there is the great red cloak. With its warm colour and shape, it offers a welcome place where it is good to be. It brought to Henri's mind Jesus' words about God's maternal love: "Jerusalem, Jerusalem... how often have I longed to gather your children, as a hen gathers her chicks under her wings, and you refused" (Matt 23:37f). Every time Henri looked at the tent-like and wing-like cloak in the painting his heart begins to sing in the words of the Psalmist:

> "You who dwell in the shelter of the Most High
> and abide in the shade of the Almighty –
> say to your God: "My refuge, my stronghold,
> my God in whom I trust
> ...You'd conceal me with your pinions
> and under your wings, I shall find refuge"
>
> (Ps 91:1-4)

The father in Rembrandt's painting is blind, but now he sees with an inner eye, the spiritual eye of love. In the face of love Henri comes to the core of his own spiritual struggle. He has to struggle against self-rejection, self-contempt and self-loathing. It is easier than one thinks not to love and accept ourselves.

He recalls once when he met a young man who was loved and admired by anyone who knew him. He told Henri about how a small critical remark from one of his friends threw him into an abyss of depression. He felt his friend had broken his wall of defenses and had seen him as he really was: an ugly hypocrite, a despicable man. For years he walked around with inner questions: "Does anyone really love me? Does anybody care?" Every time he succeeded he had the thought: "This is not who I really am: one day everything will come crashing down and the people will see that I am no good" (p. 108). We often spend time like Henri's friend wondering if we are truly loved and accepted. Faith is the courage to accept that I am loved and cherished. The Parable of the Prodigal and Rembrandt's interpretation of it shows us the love of God which is even greater than that of a mother and father. God is greater than both. Rembrandt lets us see this love.

In the Parable the father calls for his son to be given shoes. For farm people getting shoes signifies a passage out of poverty. The father dresses his son. The prophet Zechariah shows the significance of this investiture:

> Yahweh showed me the high priest Joshua standing before the angel of Yahweh... Now Joshua was dressed in dirty clothes as he stood before the angel. The latter then spoke as follows to those who were standing before him. "Take off his dirty clothes and dress him in splendid robes and put a turban on his head." So they put a turban on his head and dressed him in clean clothes, while the angel of Yahweh stood by and said, "You see, I have taken your guilt away." The angel of Yahweh then made this declaration to Joshua: "Yahweh Sabaoth says this, 'If you walk in my ways and keep my ordinances, you shall govern my house, you shall watch over my courts, and I will give you free access among those in attendance here... So listen, High Priest Joshua... I shall remove this country's guilt in a single day. On that day ... invite each other to come under your vine and your fig tree.' "
>
> (Zech 3:1-10)

The father throws a party for his son. At the close of the New Testament God's ultimate victory is described as a splendid wedding feast: "The reign of the Lord our God almighty has begun; let us be glad and joyful and give glory to God because this is the time for the marriage of the Lamb ... blessed are those who are invited to the wedding feast of the Lamb" (Rev 19:6-9).

Loneliness and Solitude:

We spend most of our lives running from loneliness and by continued activity think we can escape. However that inner voice inside us telling us we are worthless nags us. In Henri's work "The Way of the Heart"[21] Nouwen tells the story of St. Anthony of the Desert. Born around 251, Anthony was the son of Egyptian peasants. When he was about eighteen he heard the Gospel words "Go and sell what you own and give the money to the poor... then come and follow me" (Matt 19:21). Anthony knew these words called to him to respond. He withdrew to the desert where for twenty years he lived in complete solitude. The shell of his superficial securities was cracked and the abyss of iniquity that was possible in him was exposed. He came through this struggle by his self-surrender to the love of God revealed in Jesus. People flocked to him for healing, comfort and direction. We are not asked to imitate Anthony but we can learn from his wisdom. He accepted his loneliness and waited until he came to know the love of God poured "into his heart by the Holy Spirit given us" (Rom 5:5). This is what we can do, accept our loneliness and weakness and there meet the living God.

Our society is not a community radiated with the love of God. There is much domination and manipulation. We need to learn from Anthony. We need to come to a quiet place and be silent. We will face our insecurities and loneliness. There we learn to be silent and wait to hear the gentle voice that tells us we are beloved. We learn to have the courage to accept that we are loved. Our loneliness can be turned into a solitude, that quiet place where we know that God is present and we are present to him. One of the ways Henri did this was his "gazing" on the painting of "The Return of the Prodigal Son" by Rembrandt.

[21] Henri J. M. Nouwen, The Way of the Heart: The Spirituality of the Desert Fathers and Mothers (London: 1981), p. 5f.

Chapter 4

Vincent and Compassion:

Luke 6:36 reads: "Be compassionate just as your Father is compassionate". The word for compassionate in Greek is oiktírmōn which has its root in the Greek verb 'oktírō' which means to be sympathetic. It also denotes divine mercy. Sometimes Luke 6:36 is rendered in English as "Be merciful just as your Father is merciful".

Henri Nouwen looked at 'Compassion' with Donald P. McNeill and Douglas A. Morrison in their work *Compassion: A Reflection on the Christian Life* (New York: 1982). The word compassion evokes positive feelings. We like to think of ourselves as basically good, understanding, compassionate people. We identify being compassionate with being human. Yet at the same time humanity is torn by conflict, war, hatred and oppression. There are so many in our midst who suffer from hunger, cold and lack of shelter. Differences in race, sex, religion prevent us from honouring each other. The word compassion means "to suffer with". Compassion asks us to go where it hurts, to enter into places of pain, to share the brokenness, fear, confusion and anguish of so many. Compassion is actually a virtue found relatively little in practice. We have to look beyond ourselves to the Compassionate One, the God of Love. God chose to be with us in Jesus. God is not a stranger to us but is with us in our trials. He is close to us, closer than we are to ourselves but we live in fear and hurt and do not acknowledge that loving Presence that is with us and within us. In Philippians we read:

> "Who, being in very nature God,
> did not consider equality with God something to be used to
> his own advantage;
> rather, he made himself nothing
> by taking the very nature of a servant,
> being made in human likeness.
> And being found in appearance as a man,

he humbled himself
by becoming obedient to death—
even death on a cross!
Therefore God exalted him to the highest place
and gave him the name that is above every name,
that at the name of Jesus every knee should bow,
in heaven and on earth and under the earth,
and every tongue acknowledge that Jesus Christ is Lord,
to the glory of God the Father."

(Philippians 2:6-11)

Jesus came and revealed God's compassion to us. He calls us to be one with him and live compassionate lives. We witness to God's compassion by the way we live and work together. Paul says in the Letter to the Romans: "Do not model yourselves on the behavior of the world around you, but let your behaviour change, modeled by your new mind. This is the only way to discover the will of God and know what is good, what it is that God wants, what is the perfect thing to do" (Rom 12:3).

Henri taught at Yale between 1971 and 1981. His area was pastoral theology. One of his courses was on compassion and he taught this course using the work of Vincent Van Gogh (1853-1890). Vincent was born into an upper-middle-class family. As a child he was serious, quiet and thoughtful. His father was a minister. As a young man Van Gogh worked as an art dealer, often traveling. He became depressed after he was transferred to London. He turned to religion and spent time as a missionary in Southern Belgium. He suffered with the people, but was considered unsuitable by his church to minister. He broke with official religion at this stage, but did not lose his faith. He suffered ill-health before taking up painting in 1881. His early works contain little of the vivid colours that distinguished his later work. In 1886 he moved to Paris. He began developing a new style. His paintings grew brighter in colour. He moved to Arles in the south of France in 1888.

However, Van Gogh had psychotic episodes and delusions. He neglected his physical health as well. He lived with Paul Gauguin for a while but in a fit of rage he severed part of his left ear. He spent time in psychiatric hospitals. After he was discharged he moved to Auvers-sur-Oise near Paris where he took his life in 1890. There is still debate as to whether he took his life or not. Was it an accident? We don't know.

Henri used to give talks on Vincent and his paintings. Once he gave a talk to a group of nuns about Vincent. He had a bandage over his ear. He noticed the nuns were uncomfortable. He asked what was wrong. Embarrassed, the reverend mother said to him that when they asked about a talk on Vincent, they meant St. Vincent De Paul, their founder, not Vincent Van Gogh.

Vincent Van Gogh identified with the 'man of sorrows' who shared the lot of the poor, humiliated and broken. He saw his art as showing solidarity with the broken and the outsider. In a letter to his brother Theo he said: "That does not keep me from having a terrible need of – shall I say the word – religion. Then I go out at night to paint the stars".[1] . He looked at the poverty, loneliness and rejection suffered by Jesus who gave life to those in sorrow. He saw God in nature. When he painted the 'Starry Night' he said: "When all sounds cease, God's voice is heard under the stars (At Eternity's Gate, p. 172). He saw the stars and the night sky as expressions of the love of God. He said "the moon is still shining and the sun and the evening start, which is a good thing – and they also speak of the love of God and makes one think of the words, 'So I am with you always, even to the end of the world' (Mtt 28:20)" (At Eternity's Gate, p. 174). He saw his art as consoling those who had been broken by life. It was a new way of expressing Jesus's ministry of compassion. This is where Henri got his ideas about Vincent and Compassion.

Henri and Vincent:

Carol Berry and her husband Steve attended Henri's course at Yale. Steve was studying pastoral theology. He recommended Henri's course

---

[1] Quoted in Kathleen Powers Erickson, At Eternity's Gate: The Spiritual Vision of Vincent Van Gogh (Grand Rapids: 1998) p. 148.

to his wife Carol. She wondered how could she learn about compassion from an artist who had mental health issues and frequented brothels.

Henri based the core of his teachings on the Scripture passage from Paul's letter to the Church at Philippi: "There must be no competition among you, no conceit… always consider the other person to be better than yourself" (Phil 2:3). Henri always felt that the universities emphasised too much competition, getting reports in and getting good grades. There was no time to appreciate great works of art or literature. One only looked at these mechanically to achieve good grades. In his course Henri allowed the students to "gaze" and develop a sense of wonder.

At the time Carol and Steve attended Henri's classes the Vietnam war had just ended, racial tensions were high and so was the nuclear threat. There was a great deal of violence on many levels of society. In Europe terrorist groups sprang up and many suffered. There was need for a more compassionate society, rather than one guided by hate. Compassion, Henri said, was best understood as a desire to serve and by entering into the suffering of another. To be compassionate, one had to become present to the other. One had to be willing to walk with, sit with, cry with and bind the wounds of the other. To be compassionate means one suffers with. With her husband Steve, Carol entered Henri's course on Van Gogh. Henri introduced his class "The Compassion of Vincent Van Gogh" with these words:

> Here we are – people who want to prepare for the ministry. What do we want to do as ministers? Well, one thing is sure: We want to give strength to people in their daily life struggles. Many people have done this, and we often reflect on their lives for inspiration. I should like to introduce to you a man you have often heard of but not as a giver of strength, not as a minister… It is the Dutch painter Vincent Van Gogh.[2]

---

[2] Henri Nouwen, Introduction to "The Compassion of Vincent Van Gogh" (lecture, Yale University, New Haven, CT: 1978) audiotape.

Henri's aim was to create a space and time where a true encounter with Vincent could take place. Carol wondered how could Henri hope to make his students understand Vincent's broken life and teach them about compassion. Henri said that the longer he lived and tried to make sense out of his own struggles, the more he found in Vincent a kindred spirit. When he felt lonely Vincent became his companion, someone he could identify with. Henri asked his students that if Vincent was dismissed just as a crazy person why did so many people relate to his art. Vincent loved the poor and the broken. He hoped his art would help heal those broken by life. Henri spent time in Amsterdam visiting the newly-opened Van Gogh museum and looked at Vincent's mission to use art as an expressive language. The art critic Maurice Beaubourg said: "One shouldn't look at just one painting by Mr. Vincent Van Gogh. One has to see them all to understand".[3] Vincent became increasingly aware of his art giving voice to his feelings rather than reproducing only what he saw. Henri had an encounter with Vincent's nephew, who had been instrumental in the establishment of the Van Gogh Museum. Henri asked him why did so many people, in their thousands, come to the Museum. Henri related Dr. Van Gogh's answer:

> "Because people feel comforted and consoled. Vincent was able to crawl under the skin of nature and people and find there something truthful, something beautiful, something joyful, and something worth seeing. He was able to draw out the inner secret of what he saw."[4]

Henri said that Vincent offers hope because he looks closely at people and the world and discovers the world is worth seeing. Vincent was compassionate and affirmed the humanity and struggles of people. Carol was contacted by Sister Sue Mosteller, Henri's literary executor and spiritual director after Henri's death in 1996. Sue hoped Carol could do something with the notes and material she had gathered from Henri's course and make Henri's thoughts on Van Gogh available to a wider audience. Carol produced a book called "Learning from Henri Nouwen

[3] Maurice Beaubourg, Exhibition Catalogue Number 134, Stedelijk Museum Amsterdam, summer 1955, 1.

[4] Audiotape *The Compassion of Vincent Van Gogh*.

and Vincent Van Gogh: A Portrait of the Compassionate Life (Westmont, Illinois: 2019). Carol and Steve became great friends with Henri and his course at Yale influenced Carol and Steve in their ministry. Carol summarises how Henri saw the message of compassion "in the life of his saint" (Vincent):

> Henri revealed to us in his course that when one reads Vincent's letters and contemplates his paintings, three aspects of compassion come into focus. Henri said, "When we say blessed are the compassionate, we do so because (1) the compassionate manifest their human solidarity by crying out with those who suffer, (2) they console by feeling deeply the wounds of life, and (3) they offer comfort by pointing beyond the human pains to glimpses of strength and hope."[5]

The progression from solidarity to comfort helps us explore compassion with Vincent. Henri felt that studying Vincent's life would help people grow and learn more about themselves. In his class he made space for Vincent's story to connect with his students' stories. This would allow the students and us come to accept ourselves in our struggles. Vincent's exploration of life affirms us who come into contact with him. We will also learn that we are not alone.

Part I – Solidarity: Vincent cries out with those who suffer:

Henri's course gave opportunities to gain insight into one's own struggle through the channel of a life fully revealed in art and letters: Vincent Van Gogh. He addressed questions about suffering and death, about immortality, forgiveness and redemption. He looked at poverty, loneliness and despair. He strove to understand the spiritual dimension in life. He wanted to have a clearer view of how art and religion both had the power to console. He explored how the creative experience can lead to a greater love for creation and each other. He felt within himself the impulse of the Spirit to console others. Henri's students had to learn Vincent, not as experts, but by experience of the heart. Through

---

[5] Henri J. M. Nouwen, "Compassion: Solidarity, Consolation and Comfort", America, March 13, 1976.

understanding our own inadequacies and vulnerabilities we could identify and connect with others. Henri used slides with images of Van Gogh's paintings and the correspondence he had with his brother Theo.

Theo supported vincent throughout his life. Vincent credited Theo with being responsible with Vincent for the creation of the painting "Starry Night". Over his lifetime there were 900 letters exchanged between Vincent and Theo.

Vincent's father was a respectable Calvinist parson of small country churches in the south of Holland. Vincent had failed in his career as an art dealer, so he decided to follow in the footsteps of his father. The parsonage physically set the parson's family apart from the common life of the villagers, but Vincent did not want to be apart from those he would minister to.

In one of Henri's earliest classes he showed the class a slide of a drawing by Vincent of a landscape with pollard birch trees that had been

Pollard Birches 1884

stunted (pollarded) in order to produce new, straight branches. The trees form a barrier separating two dark peasant figures silhouetted against the light background of the sky.

It is a bleak image of loneliness. Henri showed that the ministry can be lonely. By using this image Henri showed how Vincent could express a universal kind of loneliness, a loneliness he experienced. Henri called it a 'cosmic loneliness'.

Vincent failed in his attempts to become a pastor. He chose to become an evangelist missionary instead. He felt he had much love to give. He wrote to Theo:

> "Someone may have a great fire in his soul, yet no one ever comes to warm himself at it, and the passers-by see but a little smoke coming out the chimney, and continue on their way. Look here, now, what must be done, tend that inner fire, have salt in oneself, wait patiently yet with how much impatience? Wait for the hour, I say, until someone will come and sit down, to stay?"
>
> (Letter to Theo, June 1880)

Henri had experienced this sense of difficulty in achieving intimacy many times. He desired to embrace the world yet no-one seemed to listen. Even as a young boy Vincent had been drawn to those who suffer when he visited the poor with his father. He would attempt to "do unto others as you would have others do unto you " (see Matthew 7:12, Luke 6:31, Carol Berry paraphrase). When we recognise our part in suffering humanity then we can recognise the sufferings of others and be with them. Henri used the following scriptural passage to speak of solidarity and compassion.

> If our life in Christ means anything to you, if love can persuade at all, or the Spirit that we have in common, or any tenderness and sympathy, then be united in your convictions and united in your love, with a common purpose and a common mind. That is the one thing that

would make me completely happy. There must be no competition among you, no conceit; but everybody is to be self-effacing. (Philippians 2:1-3 JB)

Vincent took the following words of Saint Paul to himself: "Always consider the other person to be better than yourself, so nobody thinks of his own interests first but everyone thinks of the other people's interests instead. In your minds you must be the same as Christ Jesus" (Philippians 2:3-5). Vincent sought to find ways to respond immediately, lovingly and caringly to the pain of another human being. This is what Henri sought to do in his ministry.

Vincent spent his early years in a rural province called Brabant. He always related to the landscape and surrounds of the country of his youth. He developed a deep reverence for all of life. He would say that something permeated everything around, "Something from on High". Through nature God revealed his truth and love. After he had begun to paint he told Theo of the influence his rural past had on him.

> "Many landscape painters don't have that intimate knowledge of nature which those have who looked with sentiment at the fields from childhood on… You will say, but everyone has surely seen landscapes and figures since they were children. Question: was everyone also thoughtful as a child? Question: did everyone who saw them – heath, grassland, fields, woods – also love them, and the snow and the rain and the storm? Not everyone has done that the way you and I have; it takes a special kind of environment and circumstances that have to contribute to it, and also a particular kind of temperament and character to make it take root."
>
> (Letter to Theo, December 1882)

Vincent could be overcome by sadness and melancholy when he saw the suffering of his father's parishioners. He wrote to Theo that their father had once reassured him when he was feeling particularly down that "melancholy does not hurt but makes us see things with a holier eye"

(September, 1875). Vincent's heart was involved in what he saw. He looked at people and nature with deep love. He wrote to Theo: "Could it not be the case that if one loves something, one sees it better and more truly than if we did not love it?" (May 9, 1899). Once he began to paint he worked hard at translating this loving perception of the world and its people through the language of his art.

After leaving the small town of his birth, Vincent began a nine year odyssey through some of the largest cities in Europe – The Hague, Paris and London. He worked for the firm of Goupil & Cie, and art dealer. He explored this new world of art in these cities.

The Houseless and Hungry
Samuel Luke Fildes

When he was working in London he saw this illustration of the poor that was published in the periodical The Graphic. He saw how painting could impart a social message. Art could be imbued with meaning that could be read and interpreted. Art, like the art he saw in The Graphic, could help initiate reforms that were needed in society.

While Vincent was in London he fell in love with his landlord's daughter. His ardent feelings weren't returned and this cast him into a deep depression. He sought solace in reading his Bible and attended church, coming under the spell of the preacher Charles Spurgeon. He even preached in England. He read books by Thomas Carlyle, Ernest Renen and Thomas à Kempis (The Imitation of Christ). Ultimately Vincent lost his job with Goupil in 1876.

Vincent returned home and expressed an interest to follow in his father's footsteps. He endured another failure and had to abandon his preparatory studies. Then he chose to do missionary work. He was in good spirits and wrote to Theo:

> "Happy is he who has faith in God, for he shall, although not without struggle and sorrow and life's difficulties, overcome in the end. One cannot do better than, amidst everything in all circumstances, in all places and at all times, to hold fast to the thought of God and strive to learn more of Him; one can do this through the Bible as well as through all other things.
>
> It is good to go on believing that everything is full of wonder, more so than one can comprehend, for that is the truth; it is good to remain sensitive and lowly and meek in heart, even though one has to hide that feeling sometimes, because that is often necessary; it is good to be very learned about the things that are hidden from the wise and the educated of the world but are revealed instinctively to the poor and simple, to women and babies.
>
> For what can one learn that is better than what God has put by nature into every human soul, namely that which in the depths of every soul lives and loves, hopes and believes, unless it is wantonly destroyed?"
>
> (Letter to Theo, April 3, 1878)

He found a school that trained missionaries in Laeken, Belgium and he enlisted there. He heard of the poverty-stricken mining district in Northern Belgium called the Borinage. This is where he went. This is where he felt he could do most good. He wrote to Theo:

"You surely know that one of the roots or fundamental truths, not only of the Gospel but of the entire Bible, is 'the light that dawns in the darkness.' 'Through darkness to Light.' Well then, who will most certainly need it, who will have ears to hear it? Experience has taught that those who work in darkness, in the heart of the earth like the miners in the black coal-mines, among others, are very moved by the message of the gospel and also believe it."

(Letter to Theo, March, 1878)

He impressed the local pastor. He began to lead religious services. He was able to do this because he could speak French. The superior at the missionary school decided to support and supervise him for a six-month trial period.

The miners lived in rough conditions. The sanitary conditions in the mines were non-existent. The air in the shafts and galleries was putrid and hot. Little was done to ensure the miners safety. Medical and social aid was non-existent. Many miners were victims of mining accidents and explosions. The population was ravaged by many different ailments, including malnutrition, respiratory diseases, typhoid fever and tuberculosis. Alcoholism was rampant, causing further hardship for families.

Vincent felt he had to experience the desolation of his flock, not just to preach to them from a pulpit. He increasingly visited the miners in their homes. He shared his meagre ration of food with the hungry. Despite being worn out he often sat for hours by the bed of sick miners. He used his last shirt to dress the wounds of a miner who had been seriously hurt in the mines. The man was given up for lost, but thanks to Vincent's care the man was restored to health. Vincent tore up his bed linen to make bandages for those who had been injured. He left the relative comforts of the cottage of his host family and moved to a lowly hovel.

At the invitation of one of the miners, Vincent even entered the vertical shaft of one of the mines. He entered into the pits of hell. He experienced the world of the miner first hand. He wondered: "How can they treat God's creatures like this?"[6] The miners admired Vincent and they elected

[6] Mark Edo Tralbaut, Vincent Van Gogh (New York: 1969).

him to be their spokesperson in relation to their employers. He helped avoid violence erupting in some disputes. He made many converts.

However when a delegate of the 'Belgian Evangelisation Committee' was sent to assess Vincent's missionary work, they were appalled at finding their young representative indistinguishable from the miners he had come to serve. They thought he was too radical in his service and therefore could not remain a member of the respectable Missionary Society. Vincent was dismissed. They did not look beyond his appearance to the good he had done, the hope he brought and the number of those who came to church to hear him. Vincent became alienated from the institutional Church, but he still had his faith deep inside him.

Vincent then began to turn more to the world of art. This is one of his earlier drawings of the miners. It lacks the sophistication of his later works but it does communicate the grimness of the lives of the miners.

Miners in the Snow   1880

He began to study the works of Rembrandt. He felt that Rembrandt had succeeded in bringing the biblical parables to life in his paintings so that they were universally understood. "There is something of Rembrandt in the Gospels or something of the Gospels in Rembrandt" (Letter to Theo, June 1880). He could sense the pain behind Rembrandt's works. He saw in Rembrandt how images can be revelatory, evoke feelings, console and comfort. "Rembrandt is so deeply into the realm of the mysterious that he says things for which there are no words in any language" (Letter to Theo, October 1885). Vincent was on the road to becoming an artist.

Part II – Consolation:

When Vincent started his missionary work, he was an idealistic young evangelist eager to preach sermons and teach Bible lessons. Two years later his health was poor but he wrote to Theo "…I think and I believe and I love more seriously what I already thought, and believed and loved then" (Letter to Theo, June 1880). Deep down in his pit of loneliness Vincent had encountered the most basic force pervading human existence: love. He discovered the treasure that was buried in his own being. In the loneliest, dismal moments during his service among the miners, he sensed the divine and creative power of love. "In order to work and become an artist, one needs love… To live, work and love are actually the same" (Letter to Theo, November 18, 1881). Vincent was touched by the Spirit. The work of the artist witnesses to the world of the Spirit. He still wanted to live according to Jesus' example and words. He now looked at ways of loving and living amid all of creation. He wrote:

> "Everything that is truly good and beautiful, of an inner, moral, spiritual, and sublime beauty, in human beings, I think that comes from God.
>
> But I always think that the best way of knowing God is to love many things. Love that friend, that person, that thing, whatever you like, you will be on the right path to knowing more thoroughly afterwards; that is what I say to myself. But you have to love with a high, with a serious and

intimate sympathy, with a will, with intelligence; and you must always seek to know more thoroughly, better, and more. That is what leads to God, that leads to unshakeable faith."

(Letter to Theo, June 1880)

Vincent wanted to create works of art that would touch people in comforting ways. he intended his paintings to bring glimpses of beauty and light to those who lived in darkness and desperation. The marginalised in society would become the focus of his work.

His experience of the poor in spirit, with those who mourned, with the meek, with those who longed and thirsted for justice, with the pure in heart, with the peacemakers and with the persecuted (Matt 5:3-12) can be found in his paintings.

"Someone will have attended, for a short time only, a free course at the great university of misery, and will have paid attention to the things he sees with his eyes and hears with his ears, and will have reflected about it; he too, will finish by believing, and will perhaps learn more about it than he could say. Try to understand what the great artists, the serious masters, say in their masterpieces; God will be found there. Someone has written or said it in a book, someone in a painting."

(Letter to Theo, June 1880)

Vincent began to practice drawing while still in the cramped room of the miner's home in Cuesmes. He studied prints based on the art of Jean-François Millet. He loved his work on the sowers and those who worked in the fields. The art of sowing, for Vincent, embodied a message of hope and regeneration. Vincent practices sketching Millet's 'Sower' over and over. He was drawn to this image and its implied metaphors.

The Sower   1881

Vincent had gained experience at the "University of Misery". He headed to Brussels where he intended to attend the Académie Royale des Beaux-Arts in December 1880. By April 1881 Vincent had to return home to his parents who, by now, had moved to a new parish in Etten, another small town in the Brabant. He began to draw the people he saw in ordinary life. He explained to Theo: "Now I look at things with a different eye than I did during the time when I was not drawing yet" (Letter to Theo, September 1880).

Vincent argued with his father constantly, Vincent moved to The Hague. He found his figures to paint in the impoverished men and women of the almshouses and soup kitchens. As always, their simplicity and resignation to their lot in life moved him. He brought some of the destitute men and women into his studio, offering them shelter, some food and what little money he had.

The Prayer   1882

For a while Vincent lived with a prostitute called Sien. Vincent was attracted to her misery and privation. He hoped to give her a new life but Sien's family pressured her to return to her old way of life. She left Vincent. He had become attached to her children and they to him. This was the nearest Vincent would come to having a family life.

Rembrandt: Holy Family at Night (detail)

Vincent found images that comforted him in his loneliness. One such image was that of The Holy Family (also known as The Carpenter's Family) by Rembrandt. In this painting Rembrandt showed an old woman rocking a baby in a cradle while a younger woman reads by the light of a candle. By calling this painting 'The Holy Family', Rembrandt succeeded in relating the picture of an ordinary grandmother rocking her grandchild to the Nativity scene where Anne, the mother of Mary, is rocking the infant Jesus. An ordinary life is imbued with the holiness of a biblical story. Ordinary life is in its essence holy. All is sacred for those who have eyes to see. Vincent painted "La Berceuse" based on the figure of the grandmother in Rembrandt's painting. The model for this cradle rocker was his friend Madame Roulin.

La Berceuse 1889

Vincent saw the radiance of God's beauty in a baby's smile. This is something he experienced during his time with Sien. He wrote to Theo:

> "If one feels the need of something great, something infinite, something where one feels one can see God, one needn't go far to find it. I think I saw something – deeper – more infinite – more eternal than the ocean in the expression of the eyes of a little baby when it awakes in the morning – or laughs because the sun is shining in its cradle. If there is a "ray from on high", it could be found there."
>
> (Letter to Theo, December 10, 1882)

He painted images of sorrow many times when he was with Sien.

Weeping Woman   1882

These paintings were not an actual representation of Sien. They became a statement expressing the collective pain that many around him suffered and bore. His art achieved a symbolic character while at the same was based on a real human being. According to Vincent, if a painting had soul in it, then it was a successful and worthwhile piece of art.

Sorrow

Vincent's ambitions were founded on love. He was driven to master his drawing skills and his desire to console and ease the suffering of the people around him. "As to my feelings on how far one may go in a case where one should be concerned about a poor, abandoned, sick creature, I already told you on an earlier occasion and repeat it... as far as Infinity" (Letter to Theo, December 1883). Theo at this stage was supporting Vincent financially and would continue to do so for the rest of his life.

Vincent wanted to create art that would touch people. "Whether it is in figures or in landscapes, I do not want to express some saturated melancholy but serious sorrow. In short, I want to progress so far in my work that people will say, "that man feels deeply and that man feels tenderly" (Letter to Theo, July 21, 1882). Art was to become the main language through which he would continue his ministry. He painted people in their works. He was trying to draw "… In a word, life" (Letter to Theo, May 22, 1885). He painted 'The Potato Eaters' in 1885.

The Potato Eaters   1885

He painted this to honour the lives of ordinary people. Vincent invests one of the most common experiences of being human, a meal around a table, with sacredness. At this time Vincent's father died. Vincent then left his native country. He spent a brief spell in Antwerp, Belgium before moving to Paris where Theo lived.

Henri, in his course, pointed out how the Borinage helped Vincent find his inner spark. He emphasised that to become compassionate people one had to "live our intimate solidarity with the human condition" (Op. cit., America, March 13, 1976). He said:

> "Consolation demands that we be cum solus with [alone with] the lonely other, and with him or her exactly there where he or she is lonely and where he or she hurts and nowhere else. Consolation is… not the avoidance of pain, but, paradoxically, the deepening of a pain to a level where it can be shared."
>
> (Nouwen, op. cit., 'Compassion')

Vincent, according to Henri, wanted "to struggle as hard as he wanted to in order to come in touch with the heart of life as he saw it in the poor of spirit" (ibid).

We live in a culture of avoidance. We run from pain and stop our ears from hearing about it. This does not make pain or loneliness go away. Vincent, on the other hand, embraced his own pain and failing health at this time and sought to alleviate the pain of those around him. He wanted to be one with people in their hurts. Henri said:

> "When we say to a suffering person, "don't cry" or "things will be better tomorrow" or "don't worry", we really try to move that person to a place where he or she is not. But to console means first of all to be with someone where it hurts. And that's not very easy because how can you be with someone who hurts if you don't want to be here with your own pain. And therefore we run away from the pain instead of deepening it. We want to avoid it and cover it up."
>
> (audiotape, The Compassion of Vincent Van Gogh)

It is by accepting ourselves in our loneliness and pain that we grow to be human. To acknowledge and accept our pain, Henri says: "…that's a very hard thing to say and to feel. And still that's what I think consolation is" (audiotape, The Compassion of Vincent Van Gogh). His drawing 'Sorrow' showed he felt deeply the wounds of another human life and indeed all of humanity. His drawings show us his love and those who gaze at his work are drawn into that love. Henri concluded his talks about consolation with these words:

> "No one wants to increase his or her own pain, but rather invite the hurting person to come to a place, our own place, where the pain is less. For going down into the deep pain of another is like jumping into a bottomless abyss – not knowing if or where one will land. To grasp another's pain means letting go of our own safety limb and falling down to an unknown place. In this place we maybe won't have the answers that will help or alleviate the pain or explain it. We have to be willing to admit, then and there, down in the pit, that we too are helpless and weak and powerless. And who wants to do that, or be there?"
>
> (audiotape, The Compassion of Vincent Van Gogh)

It is precisely the point when we stopped looking for answers that we become an unconditional consoling presence.

Henri invites his students to look at 'The Potato Eaters'. Carol and her fellow students felt connected with the Potato Eaters. Henri further elaborated by describing the significance of the light shedding its hazy light over the peasants around the table. Henri said this light shining in the darkness became Vincent's symbol of love. It was a light that shed some warmth and brightness and consoled the peasants in their sombre and lonely existence, a loneliness Vincent suffered with throughout his life. Vincent also sensed an inner light in the souls of those he painted. It is here that Vincent encountered the quality of soul that pointed to the all-present power of love that unites us all. The meal was something sacred. It helps us understand the Eucharistic meal.

Part III – Comfort:

Vincent's arrival in Paris in March 1886 brought a tremendous upheaval into Theo's life. Theo's apartment began to reverberate with all the passion, enthusiasm, eccentricity and complexities that comprised

Vincent. For Theo, life became stimulating and turbulent and at other times unbearable. Vincent met with fellow artists in the cafés of Montmartre. He read the colour theories of Johann Wolfgang Von Goethe and Eugene Delacroix who said "colour has a more mysterious and perhaps a more powerful influence: it acts, as one might say, without our knowledge".[7]

At this time the art-market in Paris had became flooded with Japanese art. The manner of colour and light influenced the paintings of the avant-garde artists in Paris.

Wheatfield with Partridge   1887

Also at this time there emerged the newly invented paint tubes that eliminated the tedious mixing and grading of pigments that artists used to do in their studios. It was also the time of the Impressionists who

[7] Eugene Delacroix in The Journal of Eugene Delacroix (London: 1995).

broke with the standards of painting laid down by the French Academy of Art. The artists in Paris began to paint Parisian scenes with its parks, cafés and the many small forests dotting the countryside.

Vincent wanted to go to paint in the country. He wanted to live the lifestyle he believed the Impressionist artists exemplified: living simply and mindfully and creating an art inspired by nature. Now that he had discovered the power of vibrant colours he wanted to travel to a place there the atmosphere was bright and sunny.

February 1888 saw Vincent on a train heading south in search of a place suffused by sunlight. He arrived in Arles in the south of France. He rented a small house and he wanted to turn the house into a real artist's house where everything would have character. He also hoped that he could form a community of artists there. Vincent painted three hundred paintings during his stay in Arles. He would paint the ordinary people and nature, not the historical places in Arles.

He painted the famous Langlois drawbridge silhouetted against a blue sky. He painted the local housewives pounding their wash against the stones on the bank of theRhone river just below the bridge,

He was drawn to orchards, fields and gardens, the places where ordinary people were at work. he walked for miles and miles through the countryside shouldering his rolled up canvases and paints.

Vincent tried to catch the vitality of Spring in his canvases. He tried to show the force that empowered growth and fruitfulness. He layered rich colours thickly onto his canvases. He almost sculpted the trunks and branches of trees with his palette knife. He wrote to Theo: "…It exists, the lasting [the eternal] in that which passes [the temporal] (Letter to Theo, January, 1885). He painted the essence of what he observed in the orchards in order to reveal that the eternal was revealed in the yearly return of new blossoms. Nature was the book through which God spoke.

Bridge at Langlois   1888

Garden at Arles   1888

Now the bright sun of Provence that intensified the colours made him express pure delight and deep joy. They become odes to joy, pointing to glimpses of comfort and hope.

Images for the parables of Jesus, with their correlation of birth and rebirth are centered in Vincent's works The Sower (1888), painted in Arles, as well as Wheatfield with a Reaper (1889) and Crows over the Wheatfield (1890), (Erickson, op. cit., p. 77). In the 'Sower' the sun is a symbol for the divine. He painted the sun as golden yellow orbs flooding the skies with brilliant rays. It enlivened everything before it. This was the light Vincent helped to bring to the dark places where people suffered. For Vincent, the image of the sun was the image of the divine, the source that empowers creation. It shows us the work of the Spirit in creation and giving life.

The Sower, Arles   June 1888

The Sower, Arles   November 1888

Vincent believed there was an inexhaustible source of love and light – a light and love that can enter all the darkness of our lives. The inner beauty, the inner light, the capacity to love inherent in all people springs from that same source, the Spirit of Love. Writing to his sister Wilhelmine he used a beautiful metaphor for his belief: "what the power to germinate is in a grain of wheat, that is love in us" (Letter to Wilhelmine, October 1887). In the Sower we see the whole cycle of life, the sorrowful yet always rejoicing at new birth, death and rebirth under the golden orb of the sun. This brings comfort and hope. One of his gentle pictures was of almond blossoms. These represented a new beginning and new hope.

Almond Blossoms   1890

The colour yellow features prominently in Van Gogh's depictions of sowing and harvesting. In his painting, The Sower, Van Gogh explained his intention of representing the presence of Christ through the symbolic use of colour, particularly a golden citron-yellow:

> "This is the point. The Christ in the Boat [Christ Asleep During the Tempest] by Eugène Delacroix and Millet's Sower are absolutely different in execution. The Christ in the Boat – I am speaking of the sketch in blue and green with touches of violet, red and a little citron-yellow for the nimbus, the halo speaks a symbolic language through colour alone. Millet's Sower is a colorless gray, like Israël's pictures. Now, could you paint the sower in colour, with a simultaneous contrast of, for instance, yellow and violet?"
>
> (Letter to Theo, June 28, 1888)

Van Gogh expressed his hope while at the same time battling with depression. In the years from 1875 - 1880 Van Gogh identified with Jesus in the agony of Gethsemane and Golgotha. His struggles were about to get worse.

Eternity's Gate   1890

Paul Gauguin was the only artist to come to Vincent in his quest to form a community of artists. This was due to Theo who offered to sponsor Gauguin if he went to Arles. He stayed for three months with Vincent. They produced works of astounding beauty. Vincent painted his famous sunflowers to make Gauguin feel welcome:

Sunflowers   1889

However, the relationship between Vincent and Gauguin was stormy and unbalanced. Gauguin decided to leave and this led to the famous incident where Vincent mutilated one of his ears. Gauguin left for Paris.

Vincent checked himself into an asylum in Saint-Rémy. He suffered seizures, bouts of depression and at other times he was lucid and clear. He was allowed to paint when he was feeling a little better. One of the works Vincent produced here was the Olive Trees:

Olive Trees   1889

Vincent felt he could express the divine without depending on traditional religious images. He said: "One can try to give an impression of anguish without aiming straight at the historic Garden of Gethsemane..." (Letter to Theo, March 20, 1889). In the haunted, frightened trees we sense the loneliness of Jesus in Gethsemane. The name Gethsemane itself means 'oil-press', the oil pressed from the olives.

Van Gogh painted other religious paintings: 'The Pietà', 'The Raising of Lazarus' and 'The Good Samaritan'. He was reading about Rembrandt at the time and he tried to do his own interpretation of the Biblical texts.

The Raising of Lazarus – Rembrandt

This is Vincent's version of the raising of Lazarus:

The Raising of Lazarus   1890

The sun represents the divine, the Christ. Lazarus looks like Vincent and shows his life and courage in the midst of suffering. He depicted human suffering but there was always hope.

He painted his iconic 'Starry Night' at this stage in his life.

Starry Night   1889

This painting shows his longing for the union of the infinite, the eternal with the finite. It shows his longing for peace and the end of suffering. The 'Starry Night' is an image of divine love. Vincent said: "When all sounds cease, God's voice is heard under the stars" (Letter to Theo, September 27, 1888). "The moon is still shining, and the sun and the evening star, which is a good thing – and they also often speak of the Love of God, and make one think of the words: 'Lo, I am with you always, even to the end of time (Matt 28:20)'" (Letter to Theo, July 1877). The sky at night evoked a mystical sense in Van Gogh.

Carol Berry tells us that tending the Romanesque cloister and historic monastery, while still offering psychiatric service, promotes the idea of the therapeutic role of creating art – the 'Association Valétudo'. Vincent's dream of creating an alliance of artists who would paint and draw together has become a reality.

Upon the urging of Theo, Vincent left Saint-Rémy and headed north. He went to Auvers-sur-Oise. Vincent felt that one day he would meet God and understand how pain would be understood in a new way. He lost his life here. It was assumed to be suicide but it was possibly due to a shooting accident.

Wheatfield with Crows   1890

This was the last painting of Vincent Van Gogh. It shows agony and anguish, yet in the brightness of the wheat there is life. There is darkness there but Vincent always showed a light in the darkness. Paul Tillich, the philosopher and theologian said:

> "All arts created symbols for a level of reality, which cannot be reached in any other way. A picture and a poem reveal elements of reality, which cannot be approached scientifically. In the creative work of art we encounter reality in a dimension which is closed to us without such works."[8]

Vincent pointed to the wonder of the Spirit and showed how this love can be seen and experienced in the ordinary. His whole work was accomplished with love and expressed this love. By gazing at his works

[8] Paul Tillich, Dynamics of Faith (New York: 1957).

we, too, can enter and experience love. His works pointed, symbolically, to the divine source that could dispel the darkness and offer hope. Eugene Delacroix said: "In a painting, a mysterious bridge seems to exist between its painted subjects and the spectator's spirit" (Berry, p. 87).

Henri said in his class about Vincent: "In the midst of darkness he saw light. In the midst of ugliness he saw beauty. In the midst of pain and suffering he saw the nobility of the human heart. He saw it and he burned with desire to make others see it" (Audiotape, The Compassion of Vincent Van Gogh). Vincent's hopes and joy radiate through his painting – his golden wheat fields, the spirals of the sky in the Starry Night. He communicates to the viewer a sense of consolation and hope. He showed us that new life can emerge from brokenness. Henri said: "When people reach out to each other in mutual openness, in mutual sufferings, tensions evaporate, smiles shine through tearful eyes and the presence of something new and eternally fresh is sensed" (Compassion, article in America, March 13, 1976).

Henri spoke about comfort as the uniting of human beings to form a new strength together. He said in his course:

> "Those who come together in mutual vulnerability are bound together by a new strength that makes them into one body. Comfort does not take our suffering away, nor does it minimize the dread of being. Comfort does not even dispel our basic human loneliness. But comfort gives us the strength to confront together the real conditions of life, not as an unavoidable fate, but as an inexhaustible source of new understanding."
>
> (Audiotape)

Chapter 5

Behold the Beauty of the Lord:

Henri often showed the need for silence so that we can reconnect with our heart and hear the voice of God in our innermost being. In a work he wrote in 1974 called 'Out of Solitude'[1] he showed the tension between our desire for solitude and the demands of contemporary life. He reminds us that it was in solitude that Jesus found the courage to do God's will. Thomas Moore writes in the foreword: "We want to overcome problems and adversities and want to change at all costs. An alternative is to care for ourselves, each other and our world."

In Mark 1:32-39 we see Jesus healing the sick and the crowds coming to him. Mark tells us that "Jesus got up in the morning and left the house and went off to a lonely place and prayed there" (Mk 1:35). This is something Jesus would do regularly. In the lonely place, Jesus finds the courage to follow God's will, to hear God's words and to do God's work. He says in the Gospel of John: "By myself I can do nothing... I seek to do not my own will but the will of him who sent me" (Jn 5:30). Without our going to a lonely place we get detached from our sacred centre.

We can desire to be useful. Henri points out this can be a sign of lack of self-esteem. We want to look good in other people's eyes and for them to have a good opinion of us. "When we start being too impressed by the results of our work, we slowly come to the erroneous conviction that life is one large scoreboard where someone is listing the points to measure our worth" (p. 22). We can believe that we are only worthwhile if we have success and we can measure others by the same yardstick. We live in fear that someone will unmask the illusion we are creating and "show us that we are not as smart, as good or as lovable" as we wanted others to believe (p. 23). We run away from our self-rejection.

Henri emphasises that we need to be like Jesus and go to the lonely place and be silent. In this solitude we can allow the gentle voice of God to speak.

[1] Henri J. M. Nouwen, Out of Solitude: Three Reflections on the Christian Life (Indiana: 1974).

"It is in this solitude that we discern that being is more important than having and that we are worth more than the result of our efforts". We come to see we are loved and accepted. This enables us to come to others and see their sacredness as children of God.

In Henri's book "Behold the Beauty of the Lord" we see how he put these principles into practice as he gazed on his favourite icons and how these threw light on his favourite scripture passages.[2] Wherever Henri was he created a sacred space into which he could invite others. In 1983 Henri went to visit L'Arche, a community for people with intellectual disabilities who are the 'core-members' of the community. Barbara Swanekamp left Rublev's icon of the Trinity on the table of the room where he was staying. Over the years he visited Trosly he found the icon of Our Lady of Vladimir, Rublev's icon of the Christ of Zvenigorod and the icon of the Descent of the Holy Spirit. He guides us into praying with these icons and 'gazing upon them' (p. 17). The icons speak to the heart that searches for God.[3]

The Icon of the Holy Trinity: Living in the House of Love:

Andrei Tarkovsky was one of the film directors who made a film about prayer. He made 'Andrei Rublev' in 1969. Little is known about the actual life of Rublev. The world Tarkovsky shows is brutish and grey, populated by louts, jesters and paranoid bureaucrats. The film is anti-icon, filled not with the redeemed light of Christ but with the darkness of fallen humanity. Rublev wanders through this world muttering "only by prayer can the soul transcend the flesh". Transcendence eludes him. One wonders if there is any room for the possibility of transcendent grace.

So it goes on until the last ten minutes when the stark black and white imagery bursts into brilliant colour as the camera pores over a montage of Rublev's most famous icons. We enter a new world in which beauty usurps ugliness and hope overcomes despair. Tarkovsky focuses on streaks and

---

[2] Henri J. M. Nouwen, Behold the Beauty of the Lord: Praying with Icons (Notre Dame, Indiana: 1987).

[3] Henri consulted the following studies of icons: Paul Evdokimov, L'Art de l'Icône: Théologie de la Beauté (Paris: 1970) and Leonid Ouspensky and Vladimir Lossky, The Meaning of Icons (Greatwood, NY: 1983).

The Holy Trinity – Andrei Rublev

blocks of pigment that resemble canvases by Mondrian or Pollock. This view of the icon comes with modern technology – sharing Tarkovsky's vision is for today as much as the fifteenth century. As the camera pulls away recognisable objects begin to appear: a tree, a church, the face of Christ. Rublev's icons appear in all their splendour. Then there is a discordant note as the music breaks the silence. The icons will never escape the dank ugliness of this world. Yet nonetheless they offer a vision of the beauty of God, a vision of transcendent truth, a glimpse of God's kingdom. They exist today to remind us of that space where God is.[4]

Henri tells a story about his mother and father. They bought a picture by Marc Chagall, before he became famous. His mother loved the painting of flowers by Chagall. "Her beauty had become intimately connected with the beauty of the gentle colours of the bouquet. With my (Henri's) heart's eye I look at the painting with the same affection as my parents did and I feel consoled and comforted" (p. 11). As he came to gaze on the icons in his book he felt the same consolation and comfort.

Henri begins his meditation on the icon of the Trinity with the same question as Tarkovsky. How can we live in the midst of a world marked by fear, hatred and violence and not be destroyed by it? When Jesus prays to his Father for his disciples he responds by saying:

> "I am not asking you to remove them from the world
> but to protect them from the evil one:
> They do not belong to the world
> anymore than I belong to the world."
>
> (John 17:15-16)

We cannot escape the world we live in but we can enter the home of love which is God and live from that place. We can pray and allow God's Spirit to live and work in us. Rublev painted his icon in 1425 in memory of St. Sergius (1313 - 1392). For Henri the contemplation of this icon became a way to enter more deeply into the mystery of divine life while remaining engaged in the struggles of our world that often can be so cruel and full of hate.

As we gaze on the icon we are invited to enter into the intimate conversation that is taking place among the three divine angels. The movement from the Father towards the Son and the movement of both Son and Spirit towards the Father becomes a movement in which the one who prays is lifted up and held secure (p. 21).

[4] see Philip Zaleski, Carol Zaleski, Prayer: A History (Boston/New York: 2005), p. 275.

Henri felt the power of this icon. Once when he felt verbal prayer was impossible he felt worn out emotionally and physically. He became the easy victim of despair and fear. He spent long periods in silence before this icon. He felt in this silence his inner restlessness melt away and lifted up into the circle of love, a circle that could not be broken by the power of this world. He felt he could bring this peace and love with him wherever he went in the world. The image of the circle is used in the Country song "Will the Circle be Unbroken". This was recorded by The Nitty Gritty Dirt Band in 1972. Roy Acuff didn't like the idea of these "hippies" playing old standards. He belonged to an older generation of country singers. However, he did enter the studio and sing with "these hippies". They produced a magical performance of "Shall the Circle be Unbroken". It is a song of sadness as the singer speaks of the loneliness of the burial of his mother. It also speaks of hope:

> "Will the circle be unbroken
> By and by, Lord, by and by,
> There's a better home a-waiting
> in the sky, Lord, in the sky..."

The psalmist says "Happy are those who live in your house" (Ps 84:4). We can find our strength is the circle that will be unbroken. This vision helped me grieve and come to terms with the death of my mother.

The Russian mystics describe prayer as descending with the mind into the heart and being there in the presence of God. Prayer takes place when heart speaks to heart. The heart of God is united with the heart that prays. We are one in the Spirit.

The Son, in the centre, points with two fingers which indicates his union of the divine and human through the incarnation. The Father, on the left, encourages the Son with a blessing gesture. The Spirit holds the same staff of authority as the Father and the Son. He points to a rectangular opening in the altar indicating that the sacrifice of the Son is for all people. The cross is an ever present reality. In modern times Dietrich Bonhoeffer, Martin Luther King, Ita Ford, Jean Donovan and Oscar Romero were martyred (p. 26). In the 21st century the number of Christian martyrs in our world is greater than at any time in history. Ours is an age of Martyrs.

Henri shows us that as we pray the icon we leave the world of fear and enter the world of love. We are affirmed as human beings and given courage. Saint Sergius, in whose honour and memory Rublev painted the Trinity icon, wanted to bring all of Russia together under the 'Name of God' so that its people could conquer "the devouring hatred of the world by the contemplation of the Holy Trinity". Henri saw Rublev teaching us the same message. He came to see that he no longer needed to be a victim of the fear, hatred and violence that rule the world. We are all invited by this icon to enter the house of love and bring it to others as we seek social justice. "Perfect love casts out fear" (1 John 4:18).

The Icon of Our Lady of Vladimir: Belonging to God:[5]

Where does our heart belong? Do we belong to the world of worries and its endless chain of emergencies and anxieties or does our heart belong to God and his ways? Henri said the icon of Our Lady of Vladimir was for him a gentle yet strong invitation to leave the compulsive milieu of the world and to enter the liberating milieu of God.

The icon is also known as "Our Lady of Tenderness". It was painted by an unknown Greek artist of the 12th century. Around the year 1183 it was brought from Constantinople to Kiev and almost twenty years later from Kiev to Vladimir.

Henri became fascinated with the eyes of Mary as he contemplated the icon. The eyes of the Madonna were not like the paintings of the Western world. She invites us with her to enter the inner life of God. Her eyes look inward to the heart of God and outward to the heart of the world, thus revealing the unity between the Creator and the creation. She sees the eternal in the temporal, the lasting in that which passes and the divine in the human. "Her eyes gaze upon the infinite spaces of the heart where joy and sorrow are no longer contrasting emotions, but are transcended in spiritual unity" (p. 33).

---

[5] Henri used Paul Evdokimov, op cit. and Egon Sendler, l'icona immagine dell'invisibile (PARIS: 1981).

Our Lady of Vladimir

The stars on Mary's forehead and shoulder speak to us of her relationship with God. She is completely open to God's Spirit. One star represents the Father, the other the Spirit. The third star is the Son. By God's will Mary gave birth to God's Son by the power of the Holy Spirit. She bears in Greek the highest title a human being has ever received: Theotokos, "The Bearer of God". All of her life is to give glory to God:

And Mary said:
"My soul glorifies the Lord
and my spirit rejoices in God my Savior,
for he has been mindful
of the humble state of his servant.
From now on all generations will call me blessed,
for the Mighty One has done great things for me —
holy is his name.
His mercy extends to those who fear him,
from generation to generation.
He has performed mighty deeds with his arm;
he has scattered those who are proud in their inmost thoughts.
He has brought down rulers from their thrones
but has lifted up the humble.
He has filled the hungry with good things
but has sent the rich away empty.
He has helped his servant Israel,
remembering to be merciful
to Abraham and his descendants forever,
just as he promised our ancestors."

(Luke 1:46-55)

Praying with the icon we learn that Mary really sees us. She sees us with the same eyes with which she sees her son, Jesus. As Mary sees Jesus she sees all her sons and daughters in him. Her eyes invite us gently to leave the house of fear and enter the house of love.

The hand of Mary invites us to come to her Son. He is the heart of the icon. Just as Jesus in his resurrection bore the wounds of his passion so Mary's heart carries the wounds she suffered "when a sword pierced her heart" (Lk 2:35). She knew what it meant to be poor, oppressed, a refugee, to be uncertain and confused about the future, to stand under the cross and experience loneliness and loss. She is now the mother of all women and men who suffer in this world. She invites us in our suffering to come to her Son. Her love and patience are always strong and persevering.

"Contemplating the child is like discovering a light that was always there but could not be seen because of previous blindness" (p. 38). A light comes from within the child. It is an inner glow of love that shines outward and deepens the intimacy between mother and child. The light illumines and gives warmth. This light giving intimacy has drawn countless people into prayerful communion with their Lord. The child holds his mother in an affectionate embrace. The mystery of the Incarnation shows us God's total, unrestricted care for humanity. The sacred image reverberates with the prayer of Jesus for his disciples:

> "When the Paraclete comes
> whom I shall send to you from the Father,
> the Spirit of truth who issues from the Father,
> he will be my witness."
>
> (Jn 15:26)

The "paraclete" is the one who comforts. The Spirit is love. Mary is the icon of the Spirit. Jesus is filled with the Spirit. We see this in his love and the inner light in the icon. The tender embrace of mother and child shows us the mystery of love between God and humanity.

The deep and lasting quality of God's love is symbolised by the heavy neck of the child. The child's neck is painted so large because it represents the Holy Spirit. 'Spirit' means breath. The Holy Spirit is the breath of God. It is he who gives life and all love comes from him. He is ever creative. This life is what Jesus offers humanity.

> "It is for your good that I am going
> because unless I go
> the Paraclete [the Spirit] will not come to you;
> but if I do go,
> I will send him to you"
>
> (Jn 16:7)

The Father is not obvious in the icon but he is the one who sent his Son. Jesus said: "I and the Father are one" (John 10:30) and "anyone who has seen me has seen the Father" (John 14:9).

Charles Péguy says of Mary after he placed his sick children under her care:

"And where arms are always so full
Because the Son has taken away all sins
But the mother has taken away all suffering"
                    (The Portal of the Mystery of Hope)

Mary loves and intercedes for all who suffer. She has taken all sorrow to herself.

The Icon of the Saviour of Zvenigorod[:6]

Andrei Rublev painted this icon of Christ at the beginning of 15th century as part of a group of icons he made for a church in the Russian city of Zvenigorod and is often called the "Saviour of Zvenigorod". The more Henri contemplated the icon the more he discovered. Behind the damaged face one sees a most tender face with eyes that show the heart of God and see humankind in search of love.

This largely destroyed icon was found in a barn in 1918 near the Cathedral of the Assumption in Zvenigorod. It was found by the restorer Vasili Kirikov by accident. As he turned over the top of one of the steps leading into the barn, he gasped with amazement at what he saw. Staring up at him was the face of the Saviour painted by Andrei Rublev. To this day, The Saviour found in Zvenigorod is called "The Peacemaker" in Russian art. It is hard to find a more suitable epithet – for almost six centuries the Saviour with a Russian face and kind, intelligent eyes expressing deep thought has been looking out on generations.[7]

Henri sees the holy face in the icon expressing God's compassion for those who suffer in an increasingly violent world. Through long centuries of destruction the face of the incarnate Word has spoken of God's mercy, reminding us that we are made in the image and likeness of God. There is an invitation in the midst of chaos: "Com to me, all you who labour and are

---

[6] Henri used mainly V. N. Lazarev, The Moscow School of Icon Painting (Moscow: 1971); M. Alpatov, Andrei Rublev (Moscow: 1972).

[7] Vasili Kirikov, The Russian Renaissance: Andrei Rublev, Soviet Life, October 1985, p 55.

Saviour of Zvenigorod – Andrei Rublev

overburdened, and I will give you rest. Shoulder my yoke and learn from me, for I am gentle and humble in heart" (Matt 11:28).

There is movement in the icon. It is as if Christ turns to look at us. Henri is reminded of when Jesus looked towards Peter and then Peter saw his own weakness and betrayal of Jesus and the love Jesus bears him: "He [Peter] went outside and wept bitterly" (Luke 22:62).

The colours are of inexpressible beauty. Various art historians have tried to describe them. Alpatov writes:

> "There is a resonance of colours, a harmony of cold blue tones with soft rose and gold.... Barely highlighted as in fresco painting, the colours are distinguished by great brightness. They harmonize with the tenderness reflected in the face."[8]

> "Red is the colour of divinity, blue of humanity. Christ the divine Word is clothed by God with humanity. The Virgin, created human, is over-shadowed by the divinity of the Spirit."[9]

Rublev's blue, for Henri, is brighter than in any other Christ image he had seen. It seemed that Rublev wanted to accentuate the humanity of Christ more than had been done in the past. The bright azure mantle helps us see clearly the warm, human face of Christ. It is endowed with

> "an irresistible charm, a gentleness in which there is no trace of Byzantine severity. Rublev's profoundly human Christ recalls the famous statue of Christ in the tympanum of the "Royal Door" of the Chartres Cathedral. Both the Russian and the early Gothic master humanize Christ to such an extent that we lose sight of the abstract, cult-like element in the representation."[10]

---

[8] Alpatov, op. cit., p. 74.

[9] V. N. Lazarev, op. cit., p. 21.

[10] V. N. Lazarev, ibid, p. 21.

Rublev's Christ has "a rare combination of elegance and strength, tenderness and firmness which expresses above all the charm of human virtue".[11]

The gaze of Jesus that looks straight at us brings to mind the words of the psalmist:

"O Lord, you search for me and you know me.
You know my resting and my rising,
You discern my purpose from afar,
You mark when I walk or lie down.
All my ways lie open to you...
O where can I go from your spirit?
Or where can I flee from your face?

(Ps 139:1-3,7)

The eyes of Christ are the eyes of God who looks with love on us. He looks at us and we feel a closeness to him. We are loved. They are the eyes of the one who sees the limitless goodness of God come into the world and sees that goodness rejected. These same eyes which look into the heart of God see the suffering hearts of God's people. In John's Gospel we see Jesus weep at the death of his friend Lazarus (John 11:36). These eyes hold "oceans of tears for the human sorrow of all times and all places. This is the secret of Andrei Rublev's Christ" (p. 56). This icon leads us to the heart of God and in this love we become more human.

Nikos Kazantzakis wrote 'Report to Greco' about his troubled spiritual search. He quotes the the following insight on the cross:

"One of the apocryphal Gospels relates how the Beloved disciple John had an astounding vision as he stood weeping before the Crucified. The cross was not of wood, but of light and crucified upon it was not a single man but rather thousands of men, women and children, all groaning and dying. The Beloved disciple trembled, unable to capture and immobilise any of the innumerable figures. All kept changing, running, disappearing; some returned a second time. Suddenly

[11] M. Alpatov, ibid, p. 74.

they all vanished and nothing remained on the cross but a crucified Cry".

(Report to Greco [London: 1973], p. 415)

The Icon of the Descent of the Holy Spirit: Liberating the World[12]

Henri reflects on how so much of our education is based on individuality. As he contemplated the icon he came to realise that we are part of a community Henri was struck by the peace of the icon. In the account in Acts (Acts 2:1-13) of the descent of the Holy Spirit, there are sudden sounds, bewilderment and amazement. Here in the icon we see tranquility, harmony and order. The icon painter wants to paint the inner event where God becomes for us the "God-within". We see twelve short rays descending from a part of a circle that represents heaven. God lives in us. Jesus says:

> "The Holy Spirit
> whom the Father will send in my name
> will teach you everything"

(Jn 14:26)

Jesus' absence is not an emptiness. On the contrary his departure has created the space in which his followers can receive the fullness of the Spirit. Jesus himself had prepared them for this:

> "It is for your own good that I am going,
> because unless I go
> the Paraclete [the Spirit] will not come to you;
> but if I do go,
> I will send him to you....
> He will lead you to the complete truth"

(Jn 16:7,13)

We enter into union with God. We live in the house of love.

---

[12] Henri used hère Paul Maratoff, Trente-cinq primitifs Russes, Collection Jacques Zolotnitzky (Paris: 1931); Ouspensky and Lossky, op. cit.; Daniel Rousseau, L'Icône, Splendour de Ton Visage (Paris: 1982).

The Descent of the Holy Spirit

The twelve rays visible at the top of the icon symbolise the fullness of the Spirit which the disciples have received. The time of confusion, misunderstanding, unbelief and fear is over. This is the Spirit of the risen Christ who fills the disciples with new hope, courage and confidence. It is the Spirit who makes them say "Jesus is Lord" (1 Cor 12:3) and cry out "Abba, Father" (Gal 4:7). It is the Spirit who helps them speak before magistrates and authorities (Luke 12:12), offers them wisdom (Acts 6:10), and guides their decisions (Acts 15:18). It is the Spirit that empowers them to continue Christ's mission of forgiving sins. Jesus promised he would be with us until the end of time (Matt 28:20). He is present with us by the power of the Spirit. The Spirit in the icon is divine love which is always with us.

The icon speaks of the call to community. It is a unity in diversity. The disciples in the painting are listening to the voice within. Each of the disciples reacts in his own way. Paul sits up straight and seems quite severe and intellectual. Peter bends over somewhat and looks more willing to listen. John inclines his head and offers affection. Matthew and Mark are eager to explain everything with their outstretched arms. They all have their own way of living and speaking the good news that we are God's children.

At the base of the icon there is a figure living in darkness. The icon reminds us that we have to reach out to those in darkness and bring light to those who dwell there. This is something that is in process. We can imagine that the darkness all around us can be total. Rejection, abuse and ignorance can blight so many of our lives. We need to enter the icon again and wait in silence for the Spirit to guide us and empower us. We are not alone, "God is with us, 'Immanuel' " (Matt 1:22-23, 28:20).

Conclusion:

Unfinished Business

When we look back at Rembrandt's 'The Return of the Prodigal Son' we feel the ending is unfinished and so it is. When we look at the icon of the Holy Spirit we see another unfinished story. Is the one in darkness released? We are called to the community of the Holy Spirit and yet we do not see this meaningful community. We are called to end the story in our own lives. In the Prodigal Son we can find ourselves in the different characters. How we respond is up to ourselves. In this sense the ending is in us.

The icon of the Holy Spirit teaches us that we often experience the opposite of the peace in the icon. We do not experience the community the icon speaks of. There is no light in the darkness. Yet we are not called to despair but to hope. We need to place ourselves in the group and allow ourselves to be open to God's Spirit. When we find God in ourselves we can reach out to others. We write the ending – 'God-in-us' is where we start. We are called, each in our own way, to find our home in the 'House of Love'.

Printed in Great Britain
by Amazon

23998241R00073